CROCHET FOR

BEGINNERS

A step-by-step guide With simple Projects. Learn How to Crochet Quickly and Easily!

Tanya Windsor Winifred

or indirect, that are incurred as a result of the use of the information contained within this document, including, but not limited to, errors, omissions, or inaccuracies.

Table of Contents

Introduction

The word crochet was created from the French term crochet meaning 'small hook'. Over the years, the crochet hook has been made from different materials such as metal, wood, bamboo, and plastic.

While there is no exact date or documentation regarding the origin of crochet, many crochet fabrics emerged during the 19th century in Europe. The research differs a bit. According to Annie Potter (n.d.), an American crochet expert, the art known as crochet goes back even further to the 16th century.

Elizabeth Grant (1893), in a journal entry dated sometime before the publication of The Memoirs of a Highland Lady referenced the first English garments made of cloth by looping yarns with a hook.

Appearing in the Dutch magazine Penélopé in the year 1823 was the first known published set of instructions for the crochet pattern for five different styles of a purse crafted from silk thread.

No matter how it got started, crochet has won its place in history. Did you know that many Irish people survived the potato famine from 1845 to 1850 because of crochet? It's true! Irish crochet saved many families who relied on their earnings from items like crocheted collars and cuffs that were produced in between their farm chores during the day and created by the light of a candle or oil lamp after dark. Many families relied on these earnings and saved them up so they could emigrate and start a new life. When they did, they brought their crochet skills along with them.

The concept of crochet began when hunters and fishermen created knotted strands of woven fibers to trap animals or snare fish or birds.

From there, handiwork expanded past the hunter/gatherer stage and progressed into personal decorations for occasions that included religious rites, celebrations, marriages, or funerals. Europe embraced the lace trimmings and incorporated them into adornments for gowns, jackets, and headpieces.

Crochet moved forward into the Victorian era, providing patterns for birdcage covers, tablecloths, purses, flower pot holders, and more. Creativity continued to add more items to the crochet world, and from 1900 to 1930, women began to design and produce afghans, sleigh rugs, teapot cozies, and hot-water bottle covers. During these years, crocheted potholders made their first appearance and flooded the hooks of every crafter.

Incorporating the methods of the past with those developed today, crochet has developed many new stitches and techniques—enough to keep a crafter busy for a lifetime!

Until the invention of written patterns and books, the artisans from yesteryear relied on copying the work of others. Samples of stitches were made and sewn onto pages that individuals kept like a scrapbook. Early patterns sometimes frustrated people trying to learn the art because, for example, an eight-pointed star through written directions might only turn out to be a six-pointed star. The reader was now always aware that besides reading the pattern, one was also supposed to use the illustration given as the more accurate guide.

Crochet can be gratifying, but impatient people might not have the easiest time adapting when they prefer instant gratification. When someone wants a new hat, you can either go to the store and buy one or:

- Find a hat pattern of something that appeals to you.
- Print, download, or buy the pattern for the hat.
- Select the proper yarn.
- Buy the yarn.
- Crochet one or more gauge swatches (more on that later).
- Crochet the hat.

If this sounds like a fun thing to do, then you'd probably enjoy crocheting. The truth is if you are a creative person that likes to keep their hands busy or just enjoys creating things, you will find that crochet could be a perfect choice.

As far as hobbies go, crochet is pretty affordable, and you can spend as little or as much as you want to. If you want to test the waters to see if this hobby appeals to you, you can buy a quality crochet hook for under $10.00 and practice with yarns available at the lower end. Once you have a better handle on the skills, you can trade up to the higher-end yarns.

Crochet is a portable hobby that doesn't take up much space, and you can do it virtually anywhere! If you're stuck on a long train commute...Crochet! Of course, you can crochet while watching TV too!

You do need some basic math skills because counting is an essential skill required in every crochet project. At a beginner level, you won't need anything beyond the ability to count. The good news is, if you work from patterns, chances are the pattern designer will have figured out all the math for you.

Once you are better practiced and want to work from stitch dictionaries and design your own projects and patterns, you might need to use a bit more math.

Best of all, it is easy to get started with crochet. I plan to introduce you to everything a beginner needs to get started. So let's get to it!

Chapter 1: Crochet is Fun!

Unlike my mother, I found great fulfillment performing handicrafts like crochet, knitting, embroidery, crewel, and counted cross-stitch. She used to tell me that she would badger her grandmother for lessons on how to crochet. After several failed attempts, my great-grandmother had had enough and said, "June, forget it."

Since I was self-taught, I had no one to tell me what I could and couldn't do. When I wanted to do something, I just went after it. When assembling this book, I found there was a lot about crochet that I never knew, even though I had been crocheting for many years. So, I am going to add things I have learned in addition to teaching you all about stitches, yarns, instructions on how to crochet, and some fun beginner patterns. Armed with all this knowledge, who knows, it may be your calling to teach other generations!

Interesting Facts About Crochet

I already shared some knowledge with you about the Irish potato famine, but did you also know:

- Crochet hook/hair dye caps still exist. I know that this is far away from doing some stitching, but if anyone remembers wearing a cap with holes in it to get some highlights in your hair, you probably recall pieces of your hair being yanked out with a crochet hook.

- The earliest crochet patterns were printed in 1824.

- Many of the early 19th century crochet hooks looked a little odd. Some of the tools from previous eras may, by today's standards, have looked a little clunky. It was common for some people to craft their hooks out of broken forks or spoons.

- A non-profit company called *Knots of Love* has donated over 340,000 hats for people who are going through chemo.

- There really are crocheted boobs! A charity group called *Knitted Knockers* provides special handmade breast prostheses for women who have gone through mastectomies or other breast procedures.

- Corner to corner is a recent crochet technique and an amazing way to create blankets.

- According to Rachel Swatman (2016), the largest crochet blanket is listed in the Guinness World Record, measuring 11,148.5 m2. The record-holder is Subashri Natarajan of India, and over 1,000 people helped combine hundreds of 40 x 40 sections. The blanket was later donated to charity.

- Yarn bombing day is June 11th. Yarn bombing is yarn graffiti and a fun way for crocheters and knitters to display their work in public places. The colorful displays are meant to reclaim cold public places and personalize them. This practice is thought to have originated in the U.S. in Texas.

- The longest chain is 130 kilometers (80.78 miles) long.

- The way a person holds a crochet hook has a name. Common names are called pencil grip, knife grip, the pinky fly hold, and the chopstick hold.

- The Granny Square is one of the oldest crochet patterns in print.

- A single wooden hand-carved modern crochet hook can cost over $100.

- The basic stitches in crochet have different names depending upon whether you are reading the U.K. or a U.S. pattern.

- The largest crochet hook is 2.77 m (9 feet, 1 inch) with a diameter of 11 cm (4.3 in) and was created in Colchester U.K., by Clare and Broa Sams.

- The fastest crocheter is from the U.S. Her name is Lisa Gentry, and she crocheted a total of 5,113 stitches in 30 minutes.

- Crochet cannot be replicated by machines.

Many Celebrities Have Enjoyed the Art of Crochet

You may not be aware that many celebrities have picked up the crochet hook and even have their own favorite patterns.

Take a peek at the list that shows stars from today and yesterday that enjoyed the craft.

- Bette Davis
- Madonna
- Aretha Franklin
- Jane Seymour
- Eva Longoria
- Vanna White
- Cher
- Martha Stewart
- Meryl Streep
- Rebecca Romijn
- Laura Ingalls Wilder
- Rose Wilder Lane
- Debra Messing
- Catherine Zeta-Jones
- George W. Carver
- Katy Perry
- Rosie Grier
- Ringo Star
- David Arquette
- Ryan Reynolds
- Scot Baio
- Susan Witting Albert
- Patricia Arquette
- Ann Bancroft
- James Buchanan

- Rebecca Bross
- Ellen Corby
- Estelle Getty
- Steven Lenhart
- Rosemary Harris
- Alyssa Milano
- Bette Midler
- Ann Sheridan
- Queen Victoria
- Olivia de Havilland

Chapter 2: What Are the Benefits of Crocheting

Besides being able to create beautiful things, were you aware that your health can benefit from crocheting? There are more benefits from crocheting than you are probably aware of. Besides the many health benefits, it can also be a great way to bond with your children when you teach them all that you have discovered. Once you have learned that crocheting can provide you with positive health benefits, you may find it a great choice for a self-care option.

Health Benefits of Crocheting

Crafts like crochet are a fun pastime, and they can keep your hands busy if you have a lot of pent-up energy. Below find some of the great benefits crochet gives you:

Ease Your Stress and Anxiety

Let's face it, we all have stress and anxiety because it has become part of daily life whether we want it or not. we need to remember to schedule in time for ourselves, and one of the best ways you can combat this is to pick up your hook and some yarn and let those creative juices flow.

It can be very therapeutic to focus on the repetitive motions of stitches and counting rows. Your mind relaxes, and your anxious thoughts will dissipate. The steady rhythm of the stitches fills your concentration, and your stress will melt away.

Crochet Helps Your Mood

If you are feeling restless and irritable, crocheting can help you through times of frustration, boredom, or feeling grumpy. The positive effects of crochet will give you a positive outlet, keeping your moods balanced.

Ease Your Grief

Loss is a horrible thing, and deep grief can make us feel as though we are unable to function. I have been there, wearing pajamas all day and unable or unwilling to get out of bed. Your world has come to an end, but using your hands to do something productive can begin to rebuild yourself. It's comforting, familiar, and inexpensive. When you feel up to it, the comfort of something familiar can help take your mind off your pain.

Crocheting Can Help With Insomnia

Insomnia can make you feel helpless. Your mind knows that you are tired, but your brain just won't turn off. Similar to easing stress and anxiety, crocheting, with its repetition and focus, can aid you in calming your mind and body enough to lull you to sleep. The next time you wake up tossing and turning, grab your crochet project and soothe your mind.

Ease Depression

When something is fun, we find it enjoyable, and our brains respond by releasing dopamine, which is a natural chemical that affects our emotions and acts as an antidepressant. When we release dopamine, we feel happier and better about ourselves.

Builds Self-Esteem

We could all use a boost to our self-esteem. By learning new skills, you can build self-esteem. Crocheting can give us a feeling of being productive and useful when we finish a project to give as a gift or use ourselves. If you sell at a craft fair, someone buying a ponytail hat from you gives you a little pat on the back for a job well done.

Working and creating a product can make you feel better, and it can help cope with the fear found in abusive relationships, being stuck at home, or unemployment woes.

Crochet Provides You With Mindfulness and Relaxation

Meditation and mindfulness have been the center of recent self-help journeys, and crochet can be a part of that for you too. Crocheting is relaxing, and performing repetitive crochet patterns helps you work your way toward inner peace. If you are looking for a way to cope, crocheting might help you find your inner self.

Crocheting Can Help You Break Bad Habits

Want to kick smoking? Do you reach for snacks too often? Crochet could help you kick your smoking habit by keeping your hands busy. If you can keep your mind on healthy avenues, you will think less of your bad habits.

Crocheting Can Improve Your Memory

According to Maddie Hiatt (n.d.), a recent survey done at the University of Wollongong Australia revealed that in women between 41 and 60 years of age, over 70% of them felt that crocheting helped improve their memory and concentration.

Reduces the Risk of Alzheimer's

I just learned this myself! Crocheting can reduce the risk of Alzheimer's by up to 50%. When you engage in exercises like crochet, it stimulates your mind and can slow down memory loss or even prevent it. Keeping your mind sharp is definitely a plus.

Crocheting Can Make You Feel in Control

If you have ever had that feeling of helplessness when you are acting as a caregiver, crocheting is a skill that makes you feel back in control. Even if you are the one struggling with an illness or injury, you get to be in control of everything, from picking your project, your color palette, or even determining the type of crochet stitches to work with. Crocheting can make a difference.

Crocheting Is Just Plain Good for Your Body!

Besides lifting your moods, crocheting can provide you with small repetitive movements that keep your eyes sharp and supples your hands, arms, and fingers.

Other Benefits

Enhances Your Creativity

Expressing your creativity can give you a lot of satisfaction, and it gives you pleasure. Making something special, especially if you designed it, will make you feel spectacular.

You Can Help Others

Want to give back to your community? You can always donate baby blankets to a nearby hospital, or your handmade crocheted toys are always welcome at a children's ward. Even making scarves for the homeless can give you a sense of satisfaction.

Bond With Your Child

If you are a parent or caregiver, teaching a child will provide you with a rewarding experience and create a lifelong bond. Children like to be creative, and learning to crochet will give them something interesting to do. It will also be a skill that they can use throughout their lifetime.

There is no specific age for a child to learn to crochet because they all learn at different paces. It might surprise you to learn that most kids can learn the basics around the age of 5 and can move on to more advanced work and patterns at 9 years of age.

Why teach a child to crochet? Below is a list of excellent reasons:

- Children learn to express their creativity in a new direction. Crochet is fun and teaches a child to use their self-expression through their color choices and project decisions.
- Learning to crochet can boost a child's self-esteem. Just like adults, children are proud of learning something new.
- Crochet hones motor skills. It might be a bit tricky at first to learn the skills, but the craft will become easier.

- Following a pattern can teach a child how to read, follow instructions, and get a grasp on basic math skills.

- Crochet is a skill without gadgets. Our children's minds are always looking at digital things like phones, tablets, and computers. There are areas of the brain that will only develop through offline stimulation.

Chapter 3: The Skills You Will Use to Get Started in Crochet

Everyone learns to crochet in their own style. It is a lifelong skill, which will allow you to make gifts for others and add beautiful touches to your own home and wardrobe. You will begin by picking out supplies that you will need to get started, learn about yarn, how to read a pattern, and then learn your first basic stitches before moving on to the more advanced ones. Everyone has different preferences, and you will quickly learn what size and style hook feels the most comfortable for you. Start simple, and before you know it, you will be a pro.

Basic Supplies You Will Need to Get Started

To get started, crochet is a very inexpensive hobby. Later when you become addicted to the fun and all the unique yarn choices, you may find it becoming a little more costly. In fact, you might even turn into a yarn hoarder like me, but let's just begin with the basic materials you will need to get started.

The basics are:

- *Crochet Hooks.* There are many types of hooks out there! I started with a beginner's set of aluminum, but there are hooks made out of bamboo, plastic, ergonomic hooks, wood, and others. As you experiment, you will figure out which hooks you like to work with the best.

- *Tapestry Needles.* These are an essential part of your start-up kit. It resembles a sewing needle, only the tip is soft, so you don't prick your fingers or split your yarn. You will use these to weave in the ends of your yarn once you tie off your finished projects.

- *Stitch Markers.* These may not be necessary when you are first starting out, but at some point, you may want these. Stitch markers are used in a couple of different ways. They can help you keep track of rows, keep track of your first stitch when working in a round, or marking things like armholes to help hold panels together when sewing.

- *Hook Case* (optional). You can hold off on this if you want, but they are mighty handy for keeping all your supplies together.

- *Measuring tools.* Keep a good tape measure and ruler at hand. You will need them to measure your gauge, and they are necessary for measuring those larger projects.

- *Small, sharp scissors.* There are many styles and manufacturers out there. Pick one that feels comfortable in your hand.

- *Yarn,* of course! Since you cannot crochet without yarn, this is a necessity. Yarn is classified by weight and fibers used, and there are many different types of yarn out there. The most common are polyester, wool, cotton, and acrylic, but there are many, many more.

Splurges:

- *Ergonomic Hooks.* These were mentioned above, but if you are new to crochet and still in the learning stages, these hooks might just tip the scales for a few extra dollars more. Many crocheters insist that this type of hook handle feels great in your hands and makes the stitching more fluid.

- *Latch Hooks.* There are some great uses for this little tool, including weaving in ends that are too short or bulky to fit in a yarn needle.

- *Pompom Makers.* What hat would be complete without a pompom at the tip? You can make them out of cardboard, but if you feel that you will be making a lot of them, go ahead and splurge on a permanently molded plastic pair.

- *Blocking Board.* This is a tool that is used for all final finishing stages of crochet.

- *Blocking Wires or T pins.* These are for pinning your project to the blocking board.

- *Scrapbook.* This can be very beneficial for a beginner, so you can keep a small swatch of stitches you have done to refer to them and any notes you might have made.

- *File Box.* This can be a storage place where you can not only keep your scrapbook but a record of your projects, complete with notes and some backup yarn samples in case you need to repair something.

- *Row Counter.* This can come in really handy when keeping track of row counts is super important, or when you are working on a stitch pattern that is difficult to keep track of.

- *Yarn Bowl.* When you get one, you are going to wonder how you ever got along without one! They keep your yarn from flopping around and falling on the floor. Some are even hand-crafted on Etsy.

- *Ball Winders*. These are nifty little gadgets that will turn a skein of yarn into little 'yarn cakes' that fit nicely into your new yarn bowl!

If you just want to practice some basic chains and stitches, you can get started for about $6 by buying the yarn and the crochet hook. If you purchase all the basics it should cost right around $30.

Holding Your Hook and Yarn

Holding a Crochet Hook

I'm sure that you're anxious to get started, but first things first, you need to learn how to hold a crochet hook. Grasp your crochet hook in your right hand just like you would a pencil because you will be holding the yarn in your left hand. should you be left-handed, hold the hook in your left hand and the yarn in your right. If you are left-handed, never fear; the instructions will always be the mirror image of whatever is described.

Holding an Afghan Hook

Grasp the afghan hook in your right hand like you would hold a paring knife. Hold your yarn in the other hand. If you wish to hold your crochet hook in this manner that is acceptable.

How to Hold Your Yarn

Wrap your yarn around your little finger, then pass it over your ring and middle finger. Draw it behind and over your index finger.

All About Yarn

When you first get started, you will probably visit your local yarn or craft store and become overwhelmed by seeing all the choices you never knew existed. Animal, plant, and synthetic fibers are all products used to create yarn.

- Animal fibers include silk, created by silkworms, wool sheared from sheep, alpaca from alpacas, angora from rabbits, and mohair from angora goats.

- Plant fibers include cotton, linen from the flax plant, and some yarns are even created from soy, bamboo, pine, corn, and some other plants.

- Synthetic fibers are man-made, and in some cases, can even be created from recycled materials. The metallic yarns are typically a synthetic, metallic-looking fiber spun in combination with another fiber.

When you are just beginning, it can be difficult to figure out which yarn is right for your project. If you are following a pattern, they might have it all right there for you in black and white, but sometimes you can be drawn to some other type of yarn. When you learn about yarn weights, it will provide you with more creative expression regarding your choices.

Tip: Another piece of information that you will find on your yarn label is a dye lot number. What this means is that yarns are dyed together in large batches and assigned a dye lot number. If you have to purchase multiples in a certain color, they should all be from the same batch because even if the color is the same, there can be subtle or not-so-subtle differences between those lot numbers.

Some synthetic man-made yarns are labeled with 'No dye lot'. The reason this particular choice is labeled this way is due to chemical processing, the production of these lots will make the exact same color every time.

The thickness of the yarn is referred to as 'yarn weight,' and it can range anywhere from super fine to super bulky. There are seven different categories of various yarn weights. The higher the number, the heavier the yarn will be, consequently the fewer stitches per inch you will get.

The majority of yarn manufacturers will make it easy for the beginner since they will have the number right there on the label stating the number and weight, but there are some manufacturers out there that don't make it as simple. If you happen to run across these, the clerks at your craft store should be able to help you obtain the right answer. In our world now, we also have this wonderful tool called the Internet, where if you Google the manufacturer, the information you seek is probably on their website.

Yarn Weights

Yarn Weight	1	2	3	4	5	6	7
Description	Super Fine	Fine	Light	Medium	Bulky	Super Bulky	Jumbo
Category	-Baby -Fingering -Sock	-Baby -Sport	-DK -Light -Worsted	-Afghan -Aran -Worsted	-Chunky -Craft -Rug	-Bulky -Roving	-Jumbo -Roving

Ply vs. Weight

This is probably confusing, but a yarn's weight has nothing to do with the scale weight. A yarn's weight describes the thickness of the strand. Any definitions of yarn weight referring to a particular ply are slowly disappearing and being replaced with the standard weight system (see above).

A 'ply' has nothing to do with weight, but if you see a pattern that calls for a particular ply, these are the general rules:

- Two-ply yarn is a super-fine yarn.
- Four-ply yarn can be bulky or of a medium-weight.
- Aran yarn is not generally referred to as a 'ply,' but this means the yarn is worsted or of medium-weight.
- There is no such thing as a one-ply yarn.

How to Read a Crochet Pattern

Once you have a handle on the basic crochet stitches (see chapter 4), you will want to learn how to read a basic pattern. As a person just starting out, you might look at all the choices out there, see the language they are written in and think they are pretty formidable. If you think it looks like it has its own language, you may be right.

Crochet patterns have their own special short-hand filled with abbreviations and terms that save space, but once you get the hang of it, the patterns become easier to read. The chart below represents the basic stitches and is fairly easy to understand.

Basic Stitch Abbreviations

Ch	chain
Sl st	slip stitch
Sc	single crochet
Hdc	half double crochet
Dc	double crochet
Tr (or trc)	triple (or treble) crochet
Dtr	double treble

These terms represent things you will do:

Inc	increase (add one or more stitches)
Dec	decrease (eliminate one or more stitches)

Turn	turn your work, so you can start the next row
Join	join two stitches together. This is usually done by using a slip stitch and working it in the top of the next stitch
Rep	repeat
Beg	beginning
Bl	block sometimes refers to as back loop
Bp	back post, meaning you work the stitch around the post rather than the loops
Cm	centimeter
Fl	front loop
Lp	loops
Rnd	round
Sk	skip
Sp	space
St	stitch
Sts	stitches
Tog	together
Yo	yarn over

Getting Started With a Typical Pattern

Now that you have had a look at the basic abbreviated terms, let's see how they relate to a typical pattern. Your pattern will be working in rows, meaning back and forth, so you form a flat piece like an afghan or work in rounds to form a piece with no seams, like a hat.

Example of a Pattern

For our example, we will use a winter jacket, which will show you what to expect when reading over a pattern and preparing for your project.

- Sizes: One size to fit bust/chest 36-38 in (91-97 cm)
- Actual Measurement: 42 in (107 cm)
- Side Length: 14 in. (36 cm) includes edging
- Sleeve Length: (measured straight from the top of the sleeve to cuff edge) 18 in. (46 cm)
- Materials:
- Quantity: 6 x 50 g balls of A, 3 x balls of B, 2 x balls of C, 3 x balls of D, 2 x balls of E, 3 x balls of F, 2 x balls of G
- Yarn: Extra Fine Merino. double knitting by Jaeger (or pure wool DK yarn with approx 137 yd/125 m per 50 g ball
- Color: 943 Raspberry A, 944 Elderberry B, 979 Tango C, 984 Violet D, 971 Loden E, 920 Winberry F, 923 Satinwood G
- Hook Size: E, F, G (3.5 mm, 4mm, 4.5 mm)
- Needle: Large tapestry needle
- 7 beads to make buttons

- Special techniques used:
  - making a foundation chain
  - increasing
  - single crochet edging
  - making button loops
  - making crochet buttons
- Gauge: Make a foundation chain of ch 37 and work approximately 6 in. (15cm) in the pattern. Block your sample and allow it to dry completely. Measure the gauge. (See chapter 8 for information on blocking and measuring gauge.) The recommended gauge for this project is 20 stitches and 10 rows to 4 inches.

If you have more stitches and rows, your gauge is too tight, and you should make a second sample using a larger hook.

If you have fewer stitches and rows, then your gauge is too loose and when you make your second sample you should use a smaller hook.

- Abbreviations:
  - ch - chain
  - sc - single crochet
  - dc - double crochet
  - inc - increase
  - st(s) - stitch(es)

The information above gives you garment sizing (sizes - sleeve length). That is providing you with specific bust measurements.

You are provided with yarn information requirements for the garment. The pattern, as in this case, tells you the number of balls you will need for each color. It also provides you with a color key.

Each pattern will include a suggested gauge for a yarn being used in the garment. When matching this gauge, your garment will come out the correct size.

Tip: Always read all the way through the pattern before you begin. Make sure that you understand all the techniques included within the directions.

***

No matter which pattern you begin with, the first thing you must do is make a slip knot on your hook. No pattern is going to tell you this. They are going to assume you are aware that everything you do begins with a slip knot. Everyone at some time has to tie their first slip knot, so let's get on with it.

The Slip Knot

There are different methods to make a slip knot. If you have never done anything with yarn, it can be a bit intimidating. By the end of this explanation, you should be a pro in no time. If you still need more of a visual example, you can probably find a video on Youtube, but here's an example:

1. Begin by holding your yarn in an arch, but leave the tail long and draped through the fingers on your other hand.
2. Twist the top of the arch clockwise.
3. Spread open the loop with two fingers.
4. Reach through your loop.
5. Pull the right strand up through the loop.
6. Continue to pull the strand up into a 'new' loop.
7. Place this loop on your crochet hook.

8. Tighten this loop on your hook by pulling on the strands.

9. Congratulations! You have just made your first slip knot, and now you are ready to move on to the next skill. You will have a lot to brag about the next time you talk to your family and friends.

With your slip knot in place on your crochet hook, you are ready to make a foundation chain, and each pattern will state the number of chains you will need before beginning on the first row.

Working in Single Crochet

So here's an example of what you might see in your pattern:

- Row 1: Ch 15; sc in second ch from hook and in each ch across

or you might see this in a different variation:

- Ch 15
- Row 1: Sc in second ch from hook and in each ch across.

You'll notice that both of these examples say exactly the same thing. When you count your chains, do not count the slip knot as a stitch. The loop on the hook will never be counted as a stitch.

Next, you will work the sc, or single crochet, in the 2nd chain from the hook and then in each of the remaining chain stitches. (Single crochet, see chapter 4). If you count your stitches (not including the loop), you should have 14 single crochet stitches.

Tip: Count stitches at the end of each row. Most patterns will tell you how many stitches you should have, and they may look something like this:

: 14 sc

(14 sc)

— 14 sc

Now you have completed Row 1. When you look at your pattern, it may say something like: ch 1, turn. What this means is that it is time to turn your work so you can make another row of stitches. That chain 1 (ch 1) is needed to raise your yarn high enough to begin the stitches for row 2. You can turn your work to the right or the left. Just make sure that you continue turning your work the same way each time you turn.

And, now you are ready to start row 2.

Some patterns may not tell you to ch 1, turn, at the end of a row, and instead, place it in the instructions for the following row. Your pattern could be written in these two different ways:

- Row 1: Sc in second ch from hook and in each rem ch; ch 1, turn.
- Row 2: Sc in each sc across.

or

- Row 1: Sc in second ch from hook and in each rem ch.
- Row 2: Ch 1, turn; sc in each sc across the row.

Working in Double Crochet

Your skipped chains and chains used to turn your work don't disappear when you work in double crochet or any of the taller stitches. Now they will count as a stitch. So let's go over some pattern examples of double crochet.

Your pattern might say:

- Ch 17.
- Row 1: Dc in fourth ch from hook and in chain across: 15 dc.

After your slip knot, you will proceed to make 17 chain stitches. Then count 4 chains away from the hook and work in a double crochet in that fourth stitch skipping those first 3 chains. You will proceed to add a double crochet in each of the remaining chain stitches. You should have a total of 15 double crochet stitches. Those last three chains will now count as your first double crochet of row 2.

When you reach the end of row 2, the pattern will tell you how many chain stitches you will need to add to raise the yarn to the height of the stitches for the following row. When doing single crochet, your one chain did not count as a stitch, but when performing double crochet, it's a taller stitch, so you will need to make 3 chains before you turn. The difference is that this set of 3 chains will act as a stitch. Going forward in double crochet, your chain of three will always count as the first dc, and you will work into the next stitch, not the first stitch.

There may be exceptions to the rule, but the pattern will always tell you if there is something different you need to know.

Parentheses, Brackets, & Asterisks, Oh My!

Besides using many abbreviations and terms, crochet patterns also utilize some symbols to tell you what to do. Crochet patterns tend to have a series of steps that repeat, so instead of repeating the same series of steps, a symbol like an asterisk (*) can be used to indicate repeats of a pattern. An example may look like this:

- Row 3: Dc in next 3 sts, *ch1, skip next st, dc in next st, rep from * across the row (or the end). What this means is that the steps following the asterisk are supposed to be repeated and kept in order until you reach the end of the row.

Another way of saying the same thing:

- Row 3: Dc in next 3 sts, *ch 1, skip next st, dc in next st*, rep from * to * across the row (or repeat each step in between the two *'s). That is just the pattern designer's way of saying exactly the same thing differently. Depending upon the author of the pattern, they may opt for a different crochet shorthand.

- Just when you think you have all this down, a pattern might want to add something else in. You may find that you will repeat steps several times within a row, only to do something completely different before the row ends.

This difference in a pattern might read like this:

- Row 3: Dc in next 3 sts, *ch 1, skip next st, dc in next st, **working a shell in the next st, rep from * across the row, ending last rep at**.

Don't get frustrated. Just take learning one step at a time. To begin with, you can ignore that ** until the pattern explains what you need to do with it. Regarding the last example, these are the steps you will work following the asterisk across the row, and at the last time, you will end at the **. What this means is that you will not work the shell the last time.

Brackets ([ ]) are used to tell you how many times to do a step. The number will immediately follow the brackets, telling you the number of times you will need to perform that certain step.

For example:

- Row 7: Dc in next 4 dc, ch 1 [sk next dc, shell in next dc] 4 times, ch 1 dc in next 4 dc. What this means is that you will work the [sk next dc, shell in next dc] 4 times before going on to work the ch 1, dc in next 4 dc.

***

Parentheses ( ) are often used in the same fashion. This symbol is used to indicate a group of stitches meant to be worked together into a stitch. For example:

in next dc work (2 dc, chr, 2 dc). What this means is that you will work all of those stitches into one dc, which will make up a shell.

The Term Working in Spaces Can Confuse the Beginner

There is one instruction that can often confuse the beginner and that is: 'work a shell in next ch sp'.

A chain space can occur when you work a chain stitch, then skip a stitch only to work into the next stitch. The space located underneath the chain, where you skipped this stitch, is where you will work in your shell. Spaces can be one or more chains. If there are three or more, they can be referred to as loops.

Working in the Round

If you are working on something like a 'granny square,' this is considered working in the round. Instructions for this type of pattern may start like this:

Ch 8, join with a slip stitch to form a ring. You start it like any other project, with a slip knot. Then you will ch 8. Insert your hook into the first chain made, then hook the yarn and draw it through the first chain and through the loop still on your crochet hook. Congratulations! You have made a small ring/circle that you will work your stitches into. When you start each row, you will need to raise the yarn to the correct height with indicated chains reflected in the pattern.

Patterns will also indicate whether you will work in the front loop or only stitch into the back loop. The front loop will be closest to you, and the back loop will be the furthest away. Examples of working in the round are found in chapter 4.

When You Begin to Work on Garments

Here is some info to save for later when you are beginning to work on clothing garments. This will help you be familiar with some of those special terms. Keep these handy for later:

- *Right front, right sleeve, right shoulder.* All of these refer to the correct body part on which the piece will be worn. Mirrored indicators will be left front, left sleeve, left shoulder.

- *Right side, wrong side.* Your pattern may indicate that you should work with the right (or wrong) side of the piece facing you. Note that the right side of a garment is the side that will be seen when it is worn.

- *Right-hand or Left-hand corner.* There may be times when you are required to join yarn in a specific corner. Depending upon your instructions, the piece will be nearest your right or left hand.

- *At the same time.* This wording is used when you are asked to work two different steps, for example, an armhole and at the neck at the same time.

- *Work same as Left (or Right) piece, reversing shaping.* This particular instruction can prove difficult for a beginner, so it should be filed away for later. But let's use the example that you have worked a series of decreases on a left shoulder. Rather than tell you exactly what to do on the right shoulder, the pattern may simply read: work same as left shoulder, reversing shaping. The pattern is really leaving it up to you to figure out what you do next. You may find it easier to put pen to paper and sketch out what you did the first time, then write the reverse for the mirrored piece.

Chapter 4: The Basics Stitches

In chapter 3, I taught you all about the simple crochet chain and covered the basics of deciphering how to read a pattern with abbreviations and symbols. Now let's go over some of the basic stitches that will get you started on your crochet journey.

The Double Chain

1. Get started by tying your slip knot and chain 3. Next, you will insert your hook into the first chain you made and draw up a loop. You should have two loops on your hook.

2. Catching your yarn with the hook, draw it through both loops found on your hook. That should leave one loop on the hook.
3. Insert your hook into the left edge strand of the double chain you just made and draw up a loop. You should have two loops on your hook.
4. Again, catch the yarn with the hook and draw it through both loops. You should have one remaining loop on your hook.
5. Continue steps 3 and 4 until you achieve the desired number of chains.

The Single Crochet (sc)

1. Perform your slip stitch and complete the desired chains for your foundation. You're now ready to work the first row of single crochet. Skip the last chain made and insert your hook into the next chain. Catch the yarn with your hook, and draw up a loop.
2. You should see two loops on your hook. Perform the yarn over the hook again and draw through both loops on your hook.
3. A single crochet stitch has now been completed, and there should be one loop on your hook.
4. Repeat these steps in each remaining chain left of your original foundation chain.
5. When you have reached the end of your foundation chain, Make 1 chain stitch and turn your work.
6. Work your sample piece in a single crochet now using the two top threads of each of the single crochet stitches from the previous row. When you insert under the 2 top threads, remember to draw up a yarn loop for a new stitch. Again, at the end of your row, chain 1 and turn.

7. To fasten off your last row on your practice piece, cut your yarn and draw it through your last loop. Tighten to keep your yarn from unraveling. If you are keeping a scrapbook to refer to, you should clip this to a page marked with what stitch it is.

Single Crochet Rib Stitch

This particular stitch has three variations. Since there are only two steps to each variation I am going to list all three below. You should try a sample swatch of each to see if you have a preference as to which variation you might want to adopt. They each have a slightly different work, and one may become your signature stitch.

First Variation

1. This variation forms a ribbed pattern. After your slip knot and your foundation chain, go ahead and perform a single row of single crochet chain one and then turn. When you begin your second row, insert the hook under only the front strand at the top of each single crochet stitch to draw up your yarn loop for your new stitch.

2. Complete each single crochet stitch in the same way, begin with a yarn over the hook and then draw through both loops. What you should see is a crochet sample with slightly taller rows, and horizontal lines will be visible on both sides.

Second Variation

1. Begin your sample piece in the same manner with your slip knot, foundation chain and first single row of single crochet. Using a similar process as variation 1, you will still form a ribbed pattern, but you will be

38

picking up only the back top strand of each single crochet stitch on any row from 2 on.

2. Yarn over and complete each stitch as before in the prior step 2. By picking up the back of the single crochet stitch, you should see a more pronounced ribbing.

Third Variation

1. Begin this sample the same as the previous two. This method combines both steps of the first and second variants.

2. On the second row of single crochet, pick up the front strand until you reach the end. Chain one, turn, and as you begin row three, pick up the back of the single crochet stitch. Alternate so your even rows use the front of the stitch and the odd rows use the back. You should notice that this creates a softer piece.

Slip Stitch

1. Begin with your slip knot and chain, however many you would like to use for your sample. For the first row only, pick up the back of the chain stitch, so you have two loops on your hook. Yarn over the hook and draw through both loops in one continuous motion.

2. When you turn for the second row and any row after, hook both strands of the stitch below, yarn over, and pull through. Your stitches should be tight and firm.

Slip Stitch Variation

1. After your foundation, work your slip stitches by inserting the hook under only the back loop of the stitch from the previous row. You will still be yarning over and drawing through the loop on the hook.

2. Continue working your swatch in this manner, and when you are done, it should resemble a knitted stockinette stitch.

Half Double Crochet

1. Begin your sample with the slip stitch chain, and then to begin working in the half double crochet, you will begin your first row by making your first stitch three chains away from your hook.
2. Yarn over and insert the crochet hook into that third stitch. Now you can make your first half double crochet by yarning over again and pulling the yarn through the stitch. You should now have three loops on your hook.
3. Yarn over one more time and pull the yarn through all three loops. That will complete your first half double crochet stitch.
4. Repeat all the steps for the half-double crochet by working across the foundation chain. When you turn your work, remember to chain 2 and make the next half double crochet in the next stitch.

Double Crochet

1. Perform your slip knot and foundation chain, chain an additional 3. Wrap yarn over your hook and insert the hook under the back loop of the chain stitch (this would be the first stitch after your chain of 3). Hook yarn and draw up a loop. (You should see three loops on your hook).
2. Yarn over the hook and draw this through the first two loops on the hook. (You should have two remaining loops on your hook.
3. Yarn over once more and draw through the two remaining loops on your hook. That will complete your

double crochet stitch, and you should have one remaining loop on your hook. Continue across the row until the end. Chain 3, turn your work, and now on the remaining rows always insert your hook under both top strands.

Double Crochet Variation

You can vary the look of your stitch by using the same variants described in the previous stitches. By using the front or the back of the stitch you can vary the look of your stitch.

A second variation is to insert your hook into the space between two double crochet stitches instead of the top of the stitch. That will produce a more open look to your double crochet stitch.

Treble

1. Perform your slip knot, then work on your foundation chain or row. Chain 4, then yarn over twice. Insert the hook into the next stitch, yarn over, and then draw up an additional loop. You should now see four loops present on your hook.
2. Yarn over and draw this through your first two loops on your hook. You should have three loops remaining on your hook.
3. Yarn over and draw this through your next two loops on the hook, leaving you with two loops remaining on your hook.
4. Yarn over once more and draw through the two remaining loops on your hook. That will complete your treble stitch, leaving one loop on your hook.
5. After finishing your row, chain 4, turn your work and begin the next row.

Rules When Turning Your Work

As we have mentioned before, when you turn your work and depending upon the stitch, you will need to add extra chains. (This is occasionally called turning chains.) What these chain stitches provide is a rise to your work so you can begin the next row.

When performing the taller stitches, these extra chains will form your first stitch for the beginning of each row. Keep this information handy or in your scrapbook.

Single Crochet = 1 chain

Half Double Crochet = 2 chains

Double Crochet = 3 chains

Treble = 4 chains

Double Treble = 5 chains

Treble Treble = 6 chains

Increasing

1. Sometimes it may be necessary to add a stitch to your work. To add a stitch, work your first stitch as normal and then make another stitch in exactly the same place.
2. You can mark the position of the addition with a contrasting color strand of yarn. If you want, you could mark the increase with a safety pin instead.
3. If you need to increase on each row, make your increase stitch on the first stitch of the previous row's addition. Continuing in this manner will make your increase stitches appear in a regular pattern. That will form a point after several rows of increasing at the same point.

You can also perform a single increase at the beginning of each row.

1. Work your turning chain as usual for the piece (see above). For a single crochet or a half double crochet, work two stitches in the first stitch of the previous row. Remember, for double crochet or any taller stitches, those turning chains will count as your first stitch. So for these stitches, you will only work one additional stitch in the first stitch of the previous row. You should see the edge of your piece slanting outward.

Increases can also fall at the beginning and end of your rows.

1. You can work the increase at the beginning of each row as above, then work your row over to the last stitch. You will work two stitches in the last stitch. By doing this, both edges will slant outward. The more frequently you use the increases at the edges, the more noticeable the degree of the slant will be.

Multiple Increases

1. If you need to add several stitches to a row, for example, a sleeve, chain the number of stitches indicated by the pattern at the end of a row. This is described as adding the chains at the end of the last row before your increase row.

2. After adding the chains for your increased stitches, you will chain the appropriate number of chains determined by the stitch you are performing, then turn your work. You will work your stitch in each of the pattern-indicated stitches. Complete the row.

Multiple Increases Added at the End of a Row

1. Work to the end of your established row, yarn over, then insert your hook under the lower-left strand of the last stitch you just completed and add another stitch.
2. Repeat this step of working a new stitch through the lower-left strand of the previous stitch. Continue steps until you have the desired number of added stitches.
3. This way of increasing produces a softer edge than the previously described one. You can also increase at either end of the row by using this method.

Decreasing

First Variation

1. If you need to decrease at the beginning of a row, follow these suggestions: Add the appropriate number of chains for turning to your piece. Skip the first stitch and work across the row to the last two stitches.
2. To decrease at the end of your row, skip the next to last stitch, then work a stitch using only the last stitch.
3. To decrease in the middle of a row, skip a stitch and work into the next one. Mark the decrease with a contrasting yarn or safety pin so you can align your other decreases accurately.
4. If your decreases are worked only at the beginning of rows, you should see your sample piece slant inward.
5. If you are decreasing at both ends of your rows, both edges will slant inward at a more pronounced degree.

Single Crochet Decrease

1. To add a decrease in the single crochet, draw up a loop in the next stitch, then draw up an additional loop in the following stitch. You should have three loops on your hook.

2. Yarn over, and in one fluid motion, draw the loop through all three loops found on your hook. So one single crochet is worked over two stitches for the decrease. Mark with contrasting yarn for the position of the decreases made within your work.

Half Double Crochet Decrease

1. To create a decrease in a half double crochet, begin with a yarn over, then insert your hook in the next stitch and draw up a loop. You should now have three loops on your hook. Yarn over and draw up a loop in the following stitch creating five loops on your hook.
2. Yarn over, and in one motion draw that loop through all five of the loops found on your hook. Mark the position of the decreases with contrasting yarn.

Double Crochet Decrease

1. In double crochet, yarn over and draw a loop in the next stitch. You should have three loops on your hook. Yarn over and draw through the first two loops on your hook, bringing the total number of loops on your hook to two. Yarn over and draw up a loop in the following stitch, creating a total of four loops on your hook. Yarn over and draw this through the first two loops on your hook. Your hook should now have three loops visible on it.
2. Yarn over once more, and in one motion draw that loop through all three loops found on your hook. Mark the position with contrasting yarn.

Treble Crochet Decrease

1. To make a decrease within the treble stitch, yarn over twice, then draw up a loop in the next stitch. You

should have four loops on your hook. Yarn over and draw through only the first two loops on your hook. Yarn over and draw through the next two loops on your hook. You should now have only two loops on your crochet hook.

2. Yarn over twice and draw up a loop in the following stitch creating five loops on your hook.

3. Yarn over and draw through the first two loops found on your hook. Yarn over and draw through the next two loops found on your hook. At the end of this step, you should have three loops on your hook.

4. Yarn over once more, and in one motion, draw this through all three loops on your hoop. Mark this position with contrasting yarn.

Decreasing Several Stitches Together

1. If you need to decrease several stitches at the beginning of a row, work a slip stitch in each stitch that needs to be decreased.

2. Slip stitch in the next stitch and chain number needed depending upon stitch. Work until the end of the row.

3. If you need to make decreases at the end of a row, simply leave the desired number of stitches unworked.

4. Make your required chains depending upon stitch, and turn your work around to crochet the next row back across the remaining stitches.

5. Should decreases need to be made within a row, for example, a neckline, work across the row to start a decrease section. Make a turning chain; if needed, refer to the information above. Turn work to complete one side of the piece. Skip the center stitches to be decreased by using your contrasting yarn. Work as the

pattern directs to complete the second side so that it matches the first.

Working in the Round

When you want to work in the round you need to understand how to work in a central method. You will need to increase the number of stitches on each row to keep your work flat or shaped depending upon the pattern directions.

A Round in Single Crochet

1. Begin with your slip knot and the required number of chains. To join this into a circle, insert your hook into the first chain on the thread.
2. Yarn over and draw it through the loop on the hook. (This is often called joining with a slip stitch.) Congrats, you have formed the foundation chain for your center ring.
3. Chain 1, then work a single crochet. To do this, insert your hook into the center hole of the ring to draw up a loop. Complete your single crochet. This will close your ring. Continue to work a single crochet around the ring until you have the required number of single crochets. This is usually about one and a half times the number of chains you made initially for the center ring.
4. Use a slip stitch to join your last single crochet stitch to the beginning chain (or to the first single crochet depending upon your directions).
5. Your center ring should be complete!

Working in Rounds With a Foundation Ring of Just 6 Chains - 5 Variations!

A Round in Half Double Crochet

1. Follow steps one and two above. Make a foundation ring of six chains.
2. Chain 2, then yarn over your hook and insert it into the ring to work a half-double crochet. Proceed by performing 11 more half-double crochet in the ring.
3. Join with a slip stitch to complete this round. Two half-double crochets will be made for each chain of the foundation ring. Remember that when working in single crochet, the beginning chain does not count as a stitch, but with the half-double crochet stitch, it will.

A Round in Double Crochet

1. Make your foundation ring as before. Chain 3.
2. Work 14 double crochets (refer to double crochet instructions).
3. Join with a slip stitch to the top of your chain 3 (first stitch).

A Round in Treble Crochet

1. Make your foundation ring. Chain 4.
2. Work 19 treble stitches (refer to treble crochet instructions).
3. Join with a slip stitch to the top of your chain 4 (first stitch).

A Round in Double Crochet Alternating With a Chain

1. Again, make your foundation ring. Chain 4. This will count as your first stitch and your first chain 1.

2. Work a double crochet, then chain 1—nine more times. Join with a slip stitch to the third chain in your original chain 4 to complete your round.

A Round in Treble Crochet Alternating With a Chain

1. Begin with your foundation ring. Chain 5. This will count as your first stitch in treble and your first chain 1.
2. Work a treble, then chain 1 — 11 more times. Join with a slip stitch to the fourth chain in our original chain 5 to complete your round.

Working in Squares

A Square in Double Crochet

1. Begin with your foundation ring of 6. Chain 3, this will be your first stitch.
2. Insert your hook in the middle of the ring, then work one double crochet stitch. Chain 3. (This will be your corner.)
3. Work two double crochets, then chain 3.
4. Repeat this two more times.
5. Join with a slip stitch at the top of the beginning chain 3.

Variation of a Square in Double Crochet

1. Start with your foundation ring of 6. Then chain 3. This will count as your first stitch.
2. Work two more double crochet stitches, then chain 2 for your corner.
3. Work three double crochets, then chain 2.
4. Repeat this two more times.

5. Join with a slip stitch at the top of your original chain 3.

A Filet Square in Double Crochet

1. Make a foundation ring of 12 chains. Chain 3. This will act as your first stitch.
2. Work three double crochet stitches in the ring, then chain 5 for your corner.
3. Work four double crochet stitches then chain 5.
4. Repeat this two more times.
5. Join with a slip stitch at the top of your chain 3 to complete your row.

Afghan Stitch

The afghan stitch is worked on a longer hook that will hold all your stitches as you work across a row. This stitch differs from regular crocheting because each row will be worked in two stages. The first step will be to draw up a loop for each stitch across the row, and then you will work each stitch off your hook as you work back to the beginning of the first row.

1. Begin with your desired number of chains. Work these more loosely than your foundation chain you have done up until now. Insert your hook into the second chain from the hook and draw up a loop. You will leave the loop you just made on the hook.
2. Continue to work your way across your foundation chain, drawing up a loop in each chain, leaving a new loop on the hook. When you reach the end of your first row, you should have as many loops as you did chains.
3. Yarn over and draw the loop through the first loop on your hook. Once drawn through, this loop will be dropped from the hook.

50

4. Yarn over and draw through two loops. That will be the new loop you just made in step 3 and the next loop sitting on your hook.

5. Repeat step 4 until only one loop remains on your hook. This loop will become the first vertical stitch for your next row.

6. When you begin your next row, skip this first stitch. Insert your hook right to left under the front vertical strand of the next stitch of your row and draw up a loop to remain on the hook.

7. Continue across working each stitch and retaining the loops on your hook.

8. Repeat steps 3 to 5 to complete the return row. Work in the afghan stitch until it reaches your desired length. When you work the last row, slip stitch in each vertical strand across the row. Tie off.

Variations of the Afghan Stitch

Afghan Stockinette Stitch

1. Make your foundation chain and work the first two rows like the previous directions for the afghan stitch.

2. Row 3, chain 1 and insert your hook from front to back between the front and back vertical strands of the next stitch and draw up a loop. This loop will stay on your hook. Repeat this across the row until you reach the end.

3. Row 4 will actually be your return row, and you will follow steps 3 through 5 as above. This afghan stitch will resemble a knitted stockinette stitch, but it will have a firmer texture.

Afghan Tweed Stitch

1. When you make your foundation chain, it will have an uneven number of chains. You will work the first two rows just as above in the afghan stitch directions.

2. For row 3, chain 1, then insert your hook from right to left through the next vertical strand so you can draw up a loop. Then you will insert your hook from left to right through the following vertical strand and draw up a loop. Be careful not to twist the yarn. Repeat this across the row until you reach the end.

3. Row 4 will again be your return row, and you will follow steps 3 through 5 as above.

4. Row 5, insert your hook left to right in the next stitch and draw up a loop taking care not to twist the yarn. Next, you will insert your hook from right to left in the following stitch and draw up a loop.

5. Repeat steps 3 through 5.

6. Row 6 will be a return row, and you will finish this off as usual. Repeat these last four rows for the pattern.

Joining in a New Color or a New Skein

You are having a great time crocheting away, and all of a sudden you run out of yarn! No worries, you can just join in with a new skein or even change colors!

It's always less noticeable to join in a new skein at the beginning or end of a row rather than in the middle. You will always want to join your yarn in the top right corner of the work (we're assuming you are a right-handed crocheter).

Whether you are adding a new color or a new skein, the process is the same: make a slip knot of the new yarn and then slip stitch it into the first stitch of the row. Any ends can be woven in later with the use of your tapestry needle.

Are you working in a round or square? No problem; just work to the end of that row, but leave the last stitch incomplete. Use the new yarn to complete the stitch, then join the round with a slip stitch worked in with the new color. Now you can continue to work the next row in the new color.

Chapter 5: Keeping You in Stitches

There are over 150 crochet stitches, and there are always new ones being invented. The longer you fill your hours with crochet, the more new things you are bound to experience. Intertwined with these stitches are different tips and techniques from around the world.

There is even a style of Japanese crocheting called Amigurumi, which is the crafting of small figures like dolls and animals that are all started in single crochet stitches.

You can even incorporate things like beads into your crochet work. Bead crochet is a technique of stringing beads onto your thread/yarn before starting your project.

Open Net Stitch

This stitch is the basis for several other pattern stitches. With its diversity, it can become filet crochet or even the background for Irish lace or other lace patterns.

1. Make a foundation chain based upon a multiple of three.
2. Row 1: Ch 5, work a double crochet (dc) in the eighth ch from your hook, *ch 2, skip the next 2 ch of foundation ch, dc in next ch*. Repeat from * to * all the way across, taking care not to twist the chain. At the end, ch 5, turn your work. (This turning ch 5 will count as your first dc and ch 2 for your next row.)
3. Row 2: Skip the first dc, dc in your next dc. * ch, dc in next dc *. Repeat from * to * across your row. You should end with a dc in 3rd ch. Ch 5. Turn your work.
4. Continue; repeating row 2 for your pattern stitch. Your sample should look like a net.

Alternating Block Net Stitch

1. Make a foundation chain based on a multiple of six plus three.

2. Row 1: Ch 5, dc in 8th ch from hook. Dc in each of the next 3 ch (first block will be made). * ch 2, skip next 2 ch of foundation ch, work dc in each of next 4 ch (this will make another block)*. Repeat from * to * across to the last 3 ch, then ch 2. Skip 2 ch, dc in last ch. Ch 3. Turn. (Your turning chain is the first stitch on your next row.)

3. Continue in rolls and alternate blocks of 4 dc (dc in dc, 2 dc over ch 2, dc in dc) with the open spaces formed by ch 2's.

Increasing in Net Stitch

At the Beginning of an Open Net Row

1. At the end of your row, work ch 5 and turn. Now you are ready for your increase row. Work a dc in the first dc of the last row (this will make 1 open space). Complete the row. If you need to increase by several squares, make three extra ch at the end of your row for each open net space you need to add. For example, if you want to add three spaces you would ch 5 (for the initial space), ch 6 more for spaces 2 and 3. Then dc in sixth ch from the hook. Ch 2, skip 2, ch, dc in sixth ch from your hook. Ch 2, skip 2 ch, dc in first dc of the last row.

At the Beginning of Alternating Block Row

1. At the end of your row, ch 5 and turn. Begin your increase row by dc in the fourth ch from your hook, dc in next ch, dc in first dc of last row (now 1 block will be

added). Complete row. If you need to increase by several blocks, make 6 extra ch at the end of the row for each extra pair (block plus open space).

At the End of an Open Net Row

1. At the end of your row, work in a ch 2, then work a double treble (dtr) in the same place where the last dc was worked. Ch 5, turn work. Work as normal.
2. To increase several open spaces, repeat the ch 2 then the dtr at the center bend of the last dtr you made. Repeat this until you have the desired number.

Diamond Net Stitch

1. Make your foundation chain with a number of chains that is a multiple of four, plus two.
2. Row 1: Sc in the second chain from your hook. *ch 5, skip 3 ch of foundation, sc in next ch stitch *. Repeat from * to * across your foundation chain without turning or twisting it. Ch 7, turn.
3. Row 2: * sc in third ch (at the center of the first chain arch), ch 5 *. Repeat from * to * across your row and end with a sc in the third ch of the last arch, then ch 2. Work dtr in the last stitch. Ch 6 and turn.
4. Row 3: Sc in third ch of first ch 5 arch. * ch 5, sc in third ch of the next arch*. Repeat from * to * across. Ch 7 and turn. Repeat rows 2 and 3 for your pattern until you reach your desired length.

Basic Chevron Stripes

Working a basic chevron pattern:

1. To maintain the peaks and troughs of the chevron stripe pattern and keep them correctly spaced, you will need to work one or more extra stitches at the

beginning, end, or both of each row. While following this pattern, you should put 2 sc stitches in the first stitch of every row.

2. When making the bottom "V" shape of the chevrons (often called the troughs), skip two single crochet stitches (skip 2 sc) at the bottom of each trough. Then continue working the next block of stitches.

3. To form the top "V" shapes of the chevrons (referred to as peaks), you will work 3 sc stitches in the same stitch (3 sc in next sc) at the top of the peaks.

When you begin your foundation chain for this pattern, it will require a multiple of 16 ch, plus 2. Using yarn A, make the required length of the foundation chain.

Row 1: This is the right side. You will work 2 sc into second ch from hook, * 1 sc into each of the next 7 ch, skip 1 ch, 1 sc in each of the next 7 ch, 3 sc into the next ch. rep from * to the end but omit 1 sc at the end of the last rep. Turn.

Row 2: Ch 1, work 2 sc in first sc, * 1 sc in each of the next 7 sc, skip 2 sc, 1 sc in each of the next 7 sc, 3 sc in the next sc. rep from * to the end and omit 1 sc at the end of the last rep. Turn.

Repeat row 2, changing yarn colors after every two rows or however many rows you choose.

You can vary the depth of any color stripe and the color sequence to give a totally new look to the basic chevron stripe pattern.

Corner-to-Corner Crochet

As mentioned previously, there are always new stitches being designed and discovered. Corner-to-corner, or as it is sometimes called C2C, is one of those new techniques and is based on various slanting brick or diamond patterns. C2C blocks are created from a combination of chain stitches and treble stitches. This technique is perfect for projects that are rectangular or square. Each block is made individually and worked diagonally while increasing with every row until the halfway point is reached.

Example of a C2C color block chart:

A	A	A	A	A	A	A	C	C
A	A	A	A	A	A	C	C	C
A	A	A	A	A	C	C	C	A
A	A	A	A	C	C	C	A	A
A	A	A	C	C	C	A	A	A
A	A	C	C	C	A	A	A	A
A	C	C	C	A	A	A	A	A
C	C	C	A	A	A	A	A	A
C	C	A	A	A	A	A	A	A

When you read a C2C chart, you begin at the bottom-right corner and make the first block. Row 1 will begin with the block to the left, and you would work diagonally up to the right. Row 3 would begin directly above, and you would follow it directly left and downward until you end up right next to the beginning of row 1. You would continue to work diagonally in this manner, changing color where indicated.

Crochet Embroidery

Have you ever dabbled in embroidery? A nice block of crochet can make a perfect background for some colorful embroidery additions. And with your embroidery, you can add beads, sequins, or other embellishments just like you would be able to in any other embroidery project. Adding them in an established pattern can even help you produce a beautiful piece of folk art. You can use cross-stitch, chain stitch, french knots, backstitch, blanket stitch, or even a satin stitch.

For example, you can use something simple like the below chart to help you cross-stitch a heart on a particular piece of crochet work:

		X	X				X	X	
	X	X	X	X		X	X	X	X
	X	X	X	X		X	X	X	X
	X	X	X	X	X	X	X	X	X
	X	X	X	X	X	X	X	X	X
		X	X	X	X	X	X	X	
		X	X	X	X	X	X	X	
			X	X	X	X	X		
			X	X	X	X	X		
				X	X	X			

					X					

Front Post Treble Stitch

A treble stitch will be taller than a double crochet stitch, and a post stitch is crocheted from the front or the back, depending upon your directions. If you are looking for a new stitch that will provide you with more texture than you previously learned in ch, sc, hds, and dc stitches, then this might be for you.

1. Ch 14, then work into the back humps of your foundation chain. DC in the third ch from your hood, then dc in each chain across. Ch 2. Turn.
2. Dc in the exact same st as the ch 2. Instead of working into the top loops of your stitches like a regular treble crochet, the front treble crochet is worked around the vertical post of the stitch.
3. Begin with yarn over twice.
4. Insert your hook from front to back to front around the post of the next stitch. Yarn over pulling up a loop (yo), pull through 2 loops 2 times.
5. Next, yarn over and draw the yarn around the back of the post and bring it up to the front on the other side.
6. Proceed by making your stitch normally, then yarn over and pull through two loops and then do that two more times.

Adjustable Rings

Ever try to make something, and when you put it together there is s hole right smack in the middle of your starting round? Well, the adjustable ring method will take care of that.

1. Form a rind with your yarn and leave a 6-inch tail. Insert the hook into the loop as if you were making a slipknot.

2. Yarn over your hook and pull through the loop, making a slip stitch.

3. Chain 1 and then sc the number of stitches indicated in your pattern instructions. Make sure that you enclose both strands of yarn that make up your adjustable ring. To close the center of the ring, pull tightly on the 6-inch yarn tail. Your first adjustable ring is complete! Yay!

4. To begin the next round of your ring, work your next stitch in the first sc of the adjustable ring. Should you need to make a semicircular shape, you will be in the outlined steps to ch 1 and turn your work so that the wrong side is now facing you. After that, you can crochet into the sc stitches of your adjustable ring and this will be indicated in your pattern.

Chapter 6: Finishing Touches

I see that you have finished your gift, but you still feel like something is missing. Isn't it wonderful that there are some edgings that you can add to add some extra pizazz to your project?

Simple Shell Stitch

Want a way to really make your crochet project stand out? The shell stitch is a fantastic way to give your project something special. The shell stitch is created using a double crochet separated by a simple chain stitch or a slip stitch.

This is a versatile edging and can be stitched around the entire border of any project. While this edging works ideally with a multiple of 6 +1, you can always cheat a little and adapt it to other projects.

You can use any yarn you want, but it is most common to use the same or similar yarn as used in your project. For a subtle look, work the edging in the same color as the project, but if you're looking for something with more pop, try out a complementary color.

So, you have tied in your new color (see chapter 4) and performed your first slip stitch. Let's begin by creating your first crochet shell.

1. Skip the next two stitches.
2. In the third stitch: dc, ch 1, rep three times, dc
3. So you should now have 5 dc stitches, and each one is separated by a ch 1. All of these will be worked into the same space.

4. Skip the next two stitches and then slip stitch into the third.
5. Skip the next two stitches and then repeat the sequence of dc, ch 1, rep three times, dc
6. Repeat steps 4 and 5 until you have worked across your row.

Crocheting Around the Corner

Maybe you have a project that you want to add this shell stitch all the way around the border. If so, you will need to know what to do when you reach the corners. It's really simple. After the final slip stitch of your initial row, chain 1 to adjust for the corner. Slip stitch into the first stitch on the new side of the work, then continue working the pattern normally up until the next corner. Always double-check your work to make sure that the number of shells on one side is the same number of shells as the other.

Cheating the Count

Normally, we should never be encouraged to cheat, but sometimes it just happens. If you are incredibly lucky or just planned your project perfectly, your sides should be factored in a multiple of 6 + 1, and your shell stitch will work out perfectly. Even if that's not the case, you can fudge your shell stitch a little bit, and there are two good ways to do this:

1. Alter the center of your row. Normally, you would want a slip stitch, skip 2, dc, ch1, rep 3 times, dc, skip two stitches, slip stitch. You may find that you need to skip more or less to achieve the correct count.
2. Slip stitch at the corners. The easier option is to simply add additional slip stitches at the beginning and end of each row, so you get the right number of stitches in the middle of your piece.

Reverse Single Crochet Edging

When an edging is added directly to a piece you have created, it is best to work a row of sc around the piece to stabilize the edges. Sc in each stitch of both the top and bottom edges, as well as the side edges. By edging the entire piece, it is more likely to keep its shape and keep the edges flat.

1. You will work a row of sc at the edge of your piece with the right side facing you. If it is a round, you may join work, but do not turn the piece. Now you will do the reverse single crochet row: * Working from left to right, begin by drawing up a loop in the next sc to the right (you should have two loops on your hook).
2. Yarn over (yo) and draw the loop through both loops on your hook (a reverse sc has now been made)*. Repeat from * to * all the way around the edge. Join and weave in the end.

Picot Edging

1. At your edge, work a row of sc. Do not turn work.
2. Picot row: Ch 1, sc in first 2 sc,* ch 4, sl st in first ch of ch 4 (you have just made a picot).
3. Proceed with sc in next 3 sc*, repeat from * to * along the first row. End with a sc in the last 2 sc.

Scalloped Edging

1. With a contrasting colored yarn, begin by working a row of sc.
2. Row 2: ch and sc in the first sc, * ch 3, then in the same place where you just worked the sc, yo and draw up a loop, yarn over and draw through the first two loops on your hook twice. You should have 3 loops on your hook.

3. Yarn over and draw through all three loops on your hook. Skip next 3 sc, sc in next sc *. Repeat from * to * working along the previous row. This produces a soft, pretty edging.

Buttons

It's true, you can make your own buttons, and those handmade buttons can add something special to your crochet projects. They are fairly easy to make, and you can use a matching yarn or something that contrasts to make a bold focus point.

How to Make a Basic Button

A lot will depend upon the size and shape of the buttons you want to create. You can use several different items or sizes and cover them with crochet. Things you can use include: wooden or plastic buttons, flat or domed buttons, or even wooden or plastic beads of various sizes. An example of covering a wooden bead is below, you may need to adjust depending upon what you choose to use.

1. Begin with ch 2 to start the spiral and then work four sc into the first chain. Don't join the round, but work 2 sc in each of the four stitches made on the previous round.
2. Continue your work in spiraling rounds of sc without joining your rounds. Shape the cover by working 2 sc into every alternate stitch until the project is large enough to cover your foundation bead.
3. Place the bead in the cover and start adding decreasing to your work. Make one sc into the next stitch, then work the next two stitches together. Repeat this until

the wooden bead is almost covered. Work every 2 stitches together until the cover is complete.

4. Fasten off the yarn and leave a 12-inch tail. Thread that onto your tapestry needle and work a few stitches to secure the end. You can use the rest of the yarn to sew it to your project.

Covered Bead

Work in a spiral of single crochet using a 4-ply sport weight yarn and a size C hook. As above, this covers a wooden bead.

Stretch-strip Cover

Work this in a flat six-stitch wide strip of single crochet. Try using DK yarn and a size E hook to cover a ¾ in wooden bead. Stretch the strip around the bead and secure it by stitching the side edges together.

Multicolor Button

You will work this option in a flat spiral of single crochet to cover the top of your foundation choice then decrease to cover the back. Variegated sock weight yarn and a size C hook will cover a 1 ¾ inch flat button with a shank.

Domed Button

Work in a spiral of hdc to cover the top of your foundation choice, then change to sc and work decrease stitches to cover the back. A good choice would be a 4-ply sport weight yarn and a size C hook. As an example, this would cover a 1 ⅜ inch domed button with a shank.

Double Crochet Rounds

Work in rounds of double crochet until your piece is large enough to fit the top of your foundation choice. Then start working in decreasing rounds of sc to cover the back. DK yarn and a size E hook are good choices to cover a 1 ¾ inch flat button with a shank.

Metallic Finish

Work a spiral of double crochet until it is large enough to cover the top of your foundation choice. After you have achieved this, you can change to hdc and decrease stitches to cover the back. Metallic yarn used with a size E hook will cover a 1 ¾ inch flat button with a shank.

Give it a try, it will take some experimentation, but you will be able to build on your skills and use novelty yarns, beads, and two-colored work to create some novel and decorative buttons.

Chapter 7: Fun Beginner Projects

What's a get-started book without projects? I have put together some fun projects that will get you started so you can have some fun.

Baby Items

Crochet Baby Blanket

Don't sweat it; even a beginner can create something suitable for a gift. This lovely blanket is created using only a single crochet and a chain stitch. Give it a soft texture by using a softer light worsted yarn. This is suitable for any level of crocheter and makes a great project for meditative purposes.

This blanket pattern will give you instructions for three different sizes: preemie, newborn, and toddler. The instructions list the smallest size first with information regarding the larger sizes in parentheses.

The measurements I have included do not have any edging factored in. If you wish to add an edge, your blanket will end up slightly larger.

Key:

- Ch: Chain stitch
- Rep: Repeat
- SC: Single crochet
- St: Stitch

What You Will Need:

- Yarn: Bernat Softee Baby Yarn - this is the recommended yarn for this project. The weight is considered 'light worsted', DK, or double knitting. Why is this information important? If you wanted to select a different yarn as a substitution, you need only look for the same weight.
- Hook: 5.5 mm I hook
- Tapestry needle
- Stitch Marker

Sizes:

- Preemie. This is the smallest size blanket and measures about 26 inches wide by 34 inches long. If you are using the suggested yarn, Bernat Softee, you will need two to three 5-oz skeins of yarn to complete the project.

- Newborn/receiving blanket. A mid-sized blanket that measures approximately 30 inches square. You can always make it a little longer, which will make it more rectangular with a measurement of about 30" x 34". You will need to have two to three skeins of Bernat Softee for this size.

- Toddler. The largest size of the blanket choices measures 36" x 44". This size requires four 5-oz skeins of Bernat Softee.

Instructions:

1. Row 1: Ch 105 (121, 145). Place a stitch marker in the first ch from your hook, then sc in 3rd ch from your hook. [ch 1, skip next ch, sc in next ch]. Rep across to the end of the row, ch 1, turn your work.

2. Rows 2: [sc in the next ch-1 ap, ch 1]. Use this sequence within the brackets and rep this across the rest of the row. At the end of the row, work a sc st into the st where you place the marker. Remove the marker if you wish before performing the stitch. Ch 1. Turn.

3. Row 3 until the end: The balance of the rows will all be exactly the same as row 2 except for one thing ... at the end of the row, work your last sc st into the turning chain of the previous row. You will repeat this row until the baby blanket reaches the length you desire.

4. Finishing off your blanket. When you have reached the length that you want, cut the yarn while leaving around six inches of extra yarn. Thread your tapestry needle with the yarn end and use the needle to weave the loose end of the yarn into the blanket. If you have any other

loose ends hanging from the blanket, now is the time to tuck them in.

This pattern works fine as is, but if you want to add additional edging there are several to choose from. The simplest is a sc that goes around the entire edge of the blanket. See chapter 6.

Cuffed Baby Booties

Key:

- Ch: Chain stitch
- SC: Single crochet
- HDC: Half double crochet
- SC Decrease: Single crochet decrease

What You Will Need:

- Yarn: Vanna's Choice® medium worsted weight yarn in two complementary colors
- Hook: 4.0 mm G hook
- Tapestry needle
- Buttons for show

Size:

- 6 - 12 months

Instructions:

1. Begin with your first color and ch 10. SC in 2nd ch from hook, sc in next 7, make 5 sc in the last ch. Now working on the second side, sc 8, join, ch 2.

2. Round 2: Hdc, 2 hdc, hdc in next 6. 2 hdc in next 2, then hdc in next 2, 2 hdc in next 2, hdc in next 6, 2 hdc, hdc in last, join, ch 1.

3. Round 3: Sc 10, 2 sc in next 2, 2 hdc in next 5, 2 sc in next 2, sc in next 10. Join. Ch 1

4. Round 4: This is performed in the back loops only - sc around. Join. Ch 1 (39 sc).

5. Round 5: This is also in back loops only - sc around. Join. Ch 1 (40 sc). Now you will change to color 2.

6. Round 6: Sc around making deep single crochets (40 sc).

7. Round 7: Begin working in both loops, sc around. Join. Ch 1 (40 sc).

8. Round 8: Sc 12, [sc decrease, sc in next 2] 4 times. sc 12. Join. Ch 1.

9. Round 9: Sc 14, dc decrease, sc, sc decrease, sc, sc decrease, sc 14. Join. Ch 1.

10. Round 10: Sc 10, 6 sc decreases, sc 11. Join. Ch 1.

11. Round 11: Sc 10, 3 sc decreases, sc 11. Join. Ch 1.

12. Round 12: Sc 10, 2 sc decreases, sc 10. Join. Ch 1.

13. Rounds 13 - 16: Sc around. Join. Ch 1 (22 sc). At the end of round 16, change color back to color 1.

14. Round 17: Sc around in new color. Join. Ch 1 (22 sc).

15. Round 18: Hdc around (22 hdc).

16. Round 19: Sc around (22 sc).

17. Round 20: Hdc around (22 hdc).

18. Round 21: Sc around (22 sc).

19. Round 22: Hdc around (22 hdc). Fasten the piece off and weave in your loose ends. Fold over the cuff (rounds 17 - 22).

As an option, you can clip stitch around the bottom of the boot to create a thicker rim. You can always sew on a cute button or even make a button out of crochet, to attach for decoration.

Accessories

Wrist Warmers

Fun to make and comfortable to wear, wrist warmers require less yarn than a pair of mittens. The beauty of this is that both the right and left are exactly the same. Choose some fun yarn and a suitable size hook and make something fun.

You will begin by creating a tube that will be wide enough to fit over your hand and wrist.

Crochet tubes are worked in the round but use only ordinary crochet hooks. Although tubes start out like a round and both are worked in a similar fashion, your end result will be different.

Working a Spiral Cylinder in Single Crochet

1. Make a required length of chain and join with a slip stitch to form a ring without twisting the chain. Work one row of sc into your chain. This will be easiest if you insert the hook into the top loop of each chain rather than into the bumps on the back. Join your round by working a single crochet into the first stitch.
2. Insert a marker into the single crochet you just worked to mark the spot that signifies the start of a new round. Continue the new round, working a sc into each stitch of your previous round.
3. When you reach the marker after working all the way around the row, do not join the round, but instead, remove the marker, work the marked stitch and replace the marker in the new stitch to mark the start of a new round. You will continue to move the marker each time you work up to it until you reach the desired length. Fasten off if there are no more instructions.

73

Working a Spiral Cylinder in Double Crochet

1. Make and join the desired length of chain stitches just like you did for the single crochet spiral. Join with a slip stitch without creating any twists in the chain. Next, chain three to begin the next round.
2. Work a double crochet stitch into each chain until you reach the end of the round. Join the first round by working a slip stitch into the third of the three initial chains.
3. Continue to work the next rounds in double crochet by starting each round with three chains and joining the round together with a slip stitch in the third of the three chains. Continue until the piece is the desired length. Fasten off if there are no more instructions.

Key:

- Ch: Chain stitch
- Sl st: Slip stitch
- SC: Single crochet
- Dc: Double crochet

What You Will Need:

- Yarn: Choose a yarn that you would like for this project. Pick your favorite color!
- Hook: Choose a hook that compliments your yarn.

Instructions:

1. Make a tube (see above) that is wide enough to fit over your hand and wrist. Begin with a round of sc, then

continue in rounds of double crochet. Make the tube long enough to fit from above your wrist to the base of your thumb.

2. At this juncture, you will stop working in rounds and begin working in rows of single crochet. Work even until the side edges of sc are long enough to accommodate the base of your thumb.

3. With the right side facing you, join again into a round and work rounds of single crochet until the tube is halfway down your fingers. Fasten off your end and darn in that loose end on the wrong side.

4. Make a second wrist warmer to match the first.

Crocheted Brioche Cowl

Brioche is closely related to ribbing. This brioche can be created in crochet by working ribbing in the back loops only.

Key:

- Ch: Chain stitch
- Dc: Double crochet
- Sl st: Slip stitch
- Fptr: front post treble

Size:

- 13 ¾ x 6 ¾ (35 x 17 cm)

What You Will Need:

- Yarn: Polaris (100% Wool/100g/39 yds/36m) Off White, three balls. You can use any super chunky yarn and comparable hook to achieve the gauge.
- 15 mm hook

Gauge:

- Using a 4x4 inch square, you should have 6 sts and five rows.

Instructions:

1. Ch 37, join with a sl st to first ch.
2. Round 1: ch 3, tr 1 in each st around. Join with a sl st to top of initial 3 ch.
3. Rounds 2 - 9: ch 2, fptr 1 in each st around. join with a sl st on top of 2 ch
4. Fasten off and weave in any ends.

Sea Breeze Tank Top Pattern

This is an easy crochet tank top pattern, and you should work this in a cotton yarn so it will be a good summer wardrobe enhancement.

The pattern is written for three adult sizes, however, you can choose to shorten or lengthen it to adapt to your personal preferences.

Key:

- Ch: Chain stitch
- St: Stitch
- Sc: Single crochet
- Dc: Double crochet
- FpDc: Front post double crochet
- BpDc: Back post double crochet

Size:

The sizing guide follows size XS (S, M, L. XL, 2XL, 3XL). E.g. Ch 32 (36, 40, 44, 48, 52, 56) means Ch 32 for XS, Ch 36 for S, Ch 40 for M, Ch 44 for L, Ch 48 for XL, Ch 52 for 2 XL, and Ch 56 for 3XL.

Tips:

If there is only one number present, for example, Ch 7, this number would apply to all the sizes.

Total number of stitches that you should have at any given time is listed between < >

DC 10 means DC into the next 10 stitches.

2DC means place 2DC into the same stitch.

Ch 2 and Ch 1 DOES NOT count as a stitch.

This top is designed for the V to fall directly in the middle of the wearer's bust area. If you are looking for the V to be higher, you should work rows 2-4 instead of rows 2-6 when creating the straps for the tank.

What You Will Need:

- Yarn: Debbie Bliss Cotton Denim DK in a pale blue or your favorite color
- 4.5 mm hook
- Darning Needle
- Scissors

Gauge:

- 10cm/4" square = 13 stitches wide x 9 rows tall in double crochet

Measurements:

Bust: 30(34, 38, 41.5, 45, 49, 52.5)

Armhole: 7.5(8.5, 9, 10, 10.5, 11, 12)

Length: 14.5(15.5, 16, 17, 17.5, 18.5, 19)

Instructions:

Left triangle:

Once you have finished your left triangle, you should hold it up to your body as the bust size can vary greatly within the same size. You may need to size up or down.

1. Foundation chain: Ch 7.
2. Row 1: Dc in the third chain from your hook. DC 4. <5>
3. Rows 2-6: Ch 2 turn, DC 5. <5>
4. Row 7: Ch 2, turn 2DC, DC 4. <6>
5. Row 8: Ch 2, turn, DC 5, 2DC. <7>
6. Row 9: Ch 2, turn, 2DC, DC 5, 2DC. <9>
7. Row 10: Ch 2, turn DC 8, 2DC. <10>
8. Row 11: Ch 2, turn, 2DC, DC 9. <11>
9. Row 12: Ch 2, turn, DC 10, 2DC. <12>
10. Row 13: Ch 2, turn, 2DC, 2DC, DC 10. <14>
11. Row 14: Ch 2, turn, 2DC, DC 11, 2DC, 2DC. <17>
12. Row 15: Ch 2, turn, 2DC, DC 15, 2DC. <19>
13. Row 16: Ch 2, turn, 2DC, DC 17, 2DC. <21>
14. If size XS fasten off.
15. Continue on for sizes: S, M, L, XL, 2XL, 3XL
16. Row 17: Ch 2, turn, 2DC, 2DC, DC 18, 2DC. <24>
17. Row 18: Ch 2, turn, 2 DC, DC 22, 2 DC. <26>
18. If size S fasten off.
19. Continue on for sizes: M, L, XL, 2XL, 3XL
20. Row 19: Ch 2, turn, 2DC, 2DC, DC until last st, 2DC into last stitch. <29>
21. Row 20: Ch2, turn, 2DC, DC until last 2 sts, 2DC, 2DC. <32>
22. If size M fasten off.
23. Continue on for sizes: L, XL, 2XL, 3XL
24. Repeat rows 19-20 until Row (22, 24, 26, 28) <38, 44, 50, 56>
25. Fasten off.

Right Triangle:

1. Foundation chain: Ch 7.
2. Row 1: DC into the third chain from your hook, DC 4. <5>
3. Rows 2-6: Ch 2, turn, DC <5>

4. Row 7: Ch w, turn, DC 4, 2DC. <6>
5. Row 8: Ch 2, turn, 2DC DC 5. <7>
6. Row 9: Ch 2, turn, 2DC, DC 5, 2DC. <9>
7. Row 10: Ch 2, turn, 2DC, DC 5, 2 DC. <10>
8. Row 11: Ch 2, turn, DC 9, 2DC. <11>
9. Row 12: Ch 2, turn, 2DC, DC 10. <12>
10. Row 13: Ch 2, turn, DC 10, 2DC. 2DC. <14>
11. Row 14: Ch 2, turn, 2DC, 2DC, DC 11, 2DC. <17>
12. Row 15: Ch 2, turn, 2DC, DC 15, 2DC. <19>
13. Row 16: Ch 2, turn, 2DC, DC 17, 2DC. <21>
14. Size XS - do not fasten off, but proceed directly to joining row instructions found below.
15. Continue for sizes: S, M, L, XL, 2XL, 3XL
16. Row 17: Ch 2 turn, 2DC, DC 18, 2DC, 2DC. <24>
17. Row 18: Ch 2, turn, 2DC, DC 22, 2DC. <26>
18. Size S - do not fasten off, but proceed directly to joining row instructions found below.
19. Continue for sizes: M, L, XL, 2XL, 3 XL
20. Row 19: Ch 2, turn, 2DC, DC until last 2 sts, 2DC, 2DC. <29>
21. Row 20: Ch 2, turn, 2DC, 2DC, DC until the last st, then 2 DC in the last st. <32>
22. Size M - do not fasten off, but proceed directly to joining row instructions found below.
23. continue for sizes: L, XL, 2XL, 3 XL
24. Repeat rows 19-20 until (row 22, 24, 26, 28). <38, 44, 50, 56>
25. Do not fasten any of these off, but proceed directly to the joining rows that coordinate with your size.

Joining Row:

1. Ch 2, turn, 2DC, 2DC, DC 18 (23, 29, 35, 41, 47, 53, 59), 2DC into the last st of RIGHT TRIANGLE. <24,29,35,41,47,53,59>

2. 2DC into the first st of the LEFT TRIANGLE, DC 18 (23, 29, 35, 41, 47, 53, 59), 2DC, 2DC. <48, 58, 70, 82, 94, 106, 118>

Body:
1. Row 1: Ch 2, turn, 2DC, 2DC, DC in each st until the last 2 sts, 2DC, 2DC. <52, 62, 74, 86, 98, 110, 122>
2. Row 2: Ch 2, turn DC in each st until the end of the row. <52, 62, 74, 86, 98. 110, 122>
3. Rows 3 - 13: Repeat row 2.
4. You can add more rows if you wish to increase the length. Please keep in mind that the ribbing you still need to add will increase the length of your piece.

Ribbing:
1. Row 1: Ch 1, turn, SC in each st until the end of the row. <52, 62, 74, 86, 98, 110, 122>
2. Row 2: Ch 2, turn, *FpDC into the next 2 sts, BPDC into the next 2 sts. Rep from * until the last 2 sts, FpDC, DC. <52, 62, 74, 86, 98, 110, 122>
3. Row 3: Ch 2, turn, DC, BpDC, *FpDC 2, BpDC 2. Rep from the * until the end of the row. DC into the second chain at the beginning of row 2. <53, 63, 75, 87, 99, 111, 123>
4. The extra DC at the end helps keep the edges of the top straight and neat.
5. Repeat all the above steps for the second side of the top.

Assembly:
1. Lay the two pieces of your tank top directly on top of each other with right sides together. Sew the straps and the sides of the top together.
2. At the bottom of each armhole (one at a time), you will insert your hook, secure the yarn, and pull up a loop.

3. Ch 1, SC evenly along the edge of each armhole, and ensure that your stitches are not too tight.
4. Sl st into the first SC to join your work. Fasten.
5. Repeat these steps for the second armhole.
6. Next, insert your hook along the V-neck and secure your yarn and pull up a loop.
7. Ch 1, SC along the edge of the V-neck. Make sure that your stitches are not too tight.
8. Sl st into the first SC to join your work. Fasten.
9. Weave in all your ends. Congratulations! You have just completed your first tank top, and I bet you will want to make more of them in other colors!

Neck Purse

A neck purse is always a handy thing to have when you want to keep your hands free. If you make it from a sparkly metallic yarn, you can even use it to go out at night.

Key:

- Ch: Chain stitch
- Sc: Single crochet
- Hdc: Half double crochet
- Sl st: Slip stitch
- St(s): Stitch(es)
- Beg: Beginning
- Rs: Right side
- Ws: Wrong side
- Incl: Including

Size:

- 4 inches square

What You Will Need:

- Yarn: Lurex Shimmer by Rowan or a viscose/polyester metallic yarn with approximately 104 yd/95 m per 25 g ball. Color A 333 Pewter
- Hook sizes: C and E
- Tapestry needle
- Small decorative button

Gauge:

Note: The yarn is going to be used doubled throughout your project, so your gauge will also be worked in double.

Using yarn A double and the E hook make a foundation chain of 33 ch and work approximately 6 inches in sc. Block your sample and allow it to dry. The recommended gauge for yarn A is 22 stitches and 24 rows to a 4-inch measurement.

Your gauge should be fairly tight because this is a stiffer type of fabric but will wear well and not easily stretch out of shape.

Instructions:

1. Using yarn A (and doubled) and the E crochet hook, work a foundation ch of 20 plus 1 turning ch.
2. Row 1: (this should be your right side) Work 1 sc in the second ch from your hook, 1 sc in each ch along your row and take care to not turn your chain (20 sc).
3. Row 2: Ch 1, work 1 sc in each sc along your row. Turn. You should have 19 sts.
4. Repeat row 2 until your work measures 8 inches in length.
5. Now you will begin to shape your flap.

6. This row should begin on the right side. Ch 1, skip first sc to decrease 1 stitch, work sc across the row. Turn. You should have 19 sc.
7. Repeat this row until only 2 sts remain.
8. Fasten off and leave a long enough tail to make a button loop.
9. Make your cord next.
10. Using yarn A doubled, and the E hook, make a foundation chain about 2 inches longer than you require. Change to the C-hook and work a row of sl st along one side of the chain.
11. Fasten off the yarn.
12. Finish your purse by using the yarn end at the point of your flap to crochet a chain long enough to accommodate the button you have chosen to use. Secure the end of the chains on the wrong side of the flap. Weave in your yarn ends and block.
13. When dry, fold up the first 4 inches with the right sides together so that your foundation chain is level with the start of your flap shaping.
14. Stitch the side edges together and turn your piece to the right side.
15. Fold over the flap on the front of the purse and mark the position of the button loop with a pin.
16. Stitch the small button and cord ends securely to your new purse. Enjoy a night out and be proud that you made your own purse. Show it off!

The great thing about this pattern is that you can play around with your sizing and custom a bag of your choosing. I used to have a bag that I could neatly tuck my paperback book in that I was reading, but I wore it out. With this pattern, I have been able to make myself a new bag, and it was so admired, that I made a few for my friends as well!

Chevron Striped Scarf

Key:

- Ch: Chain stitch
- Dc: Double crochet
- Sl st: Slip stitch
- Rep: repeat

Size:

- 10 in (25 cm) qisw, 65 in (165 cm) long

What You Will Need:

- Yarn: Recommended Legend DK by Sirdar or a wool synthetic blend of a double knitting weight yarn that has approximately 131 yd/120 m per ball.
- Colors: 626 Light Gray (A), 628 Taupe (B), 653 Naturelle (C), 621 Cream (D). Or substitute colors of your own!
- Hooks: E, F (3.5 mm, 4 mm)
- Large tapestry needle

Gauge:

- Begin with a foundation chain of 39 ch and work approximately 6 inches in the pattern, beginning with the foundation row. Block the sample and then allow it to dry. Measure the gauge. The recommended gauge for this project is 8 rows and 2 pattern repeats, adding up to 4 inches. If you have more rows or a smaller pattern repeat, then your gauge is too tight, and you should make another sample using a larger hook.

Should you have fewer rows and a larger pattern repeat, then your gauge is too loose, and you should make another sample using a smaller hook.

Instructions:

Tips: When you are making a striped scarf, it can be less daunting to deal with your yarn ends as you go instead of leaving them all until the end. Weave in the yarn ends on the wrong side of the scarf after every color change.

Always read all the way through your pattern before you begin, just to make sure you understand the techniques used.

When you are working a repeating stripe pattern, you should check after every strip to make sure that your color sequence is correct.

1. Using yarn A and the F hook, work a loose foundation chain of 52 ch. Change to the E hook to work the rest of your scarf.
2. Foundation row (which is your right side), use yarn A, and work 1 dc into the fourth ch from the hook. Then 1 dc in each of the next 3 ch, * 3 dc into next ch, 1 dc in each of the next 5 ch, rep from * two more times, 3 dc in next ch, 1 dc in each of the next 5 dc. Turn.
3. Rows 1 and 2: Sl st in second dc, ch 3 (which will count as 1 dc), 1 dc in each of the next 4 dc, * 3 dc in next dc, 1 dc in each of the next 5 dc, skip 2 dc, 1 dc in each of the next 5 dc, rep from * two more times. 3 dc in next dc, 1 dc in each of the next 5 dc, turn.

Color sequence:

- Stripe 1:End yarn A, join in yarn B and repeat rows 1 and 2.

- Stripe 2: End yarn B, join in yarn C and repeat rows 1 and 2.
- Stripe 3: End yarn C, join in yarn D and repeat rows 1 and 2.
- Stripe 4: End off yarn D, join in yarn A and repeat rows 1 and 2.

You will repeat the two-row stripes following this color sequence until the scarf measures approximately 65 inches (165 cm). End with the second sequence of stripe color 4. Fasten off yarn and weave in any ends left. Press your scarf very lightly on the wrong side on a well-padded surface.

Chicken Toys

There is something very satisfying about making cute little toys. Whether these cuties are just for your kids' Easter baskets, some cute little toys to play with, or something you donate to a children's hospital, they are sure cute.

Hen

Key:

- Ch: Chain stitch
- Sl st: Slip stitch
- Sc: Single crochet
- Hdc: half double crochet

What You Will Need:

- Yarn: All yarns will be DK weight.
  a. MC approximately 25 yds in white or brown
  b. CC1 approximately 5 yds in yellow

c. CC2 approximately 5 yds in red

- Hook: E hook
- 6 mm black plastic eyes with safety backings
- A small piece of black craft felt should you not want to use plastic eyes
- Tapestry needle
- Stuffing
- Stitch markers (optional)

Size:

- Approximately 2 ½ inches tall and 2 inches long

Instructions:

- Body
  - Using MC, make an 8 st adjustable ring (see chapter 5).
  - Rnd 1: Sc 2 in each st around. (This should be 16 st.)
  - Rnd 2: *Sc 3, sc2 in next st. Rep from * three more times (20 sts).
  - Rnd 3: *Sc 1, sc 2 in next st. Rep from * nine more times (30 sts).
  - Rnds 4 - 8: Sc 30
  - Rnd 9: *Sc1, sc 2 tog. Rep from * nine more times (20 sts).
  - Rnd 10: Sc 20
  - Rnd 11: *Sc 3, sc 2 tog. Rep from * three more times (16 sts).
  - Rnds 12 - 14: Sc 16

- ○ Stuff body.
- ○ Rnd 15: Sc 2 tog a total of eight times (8 sts). Fasten off and leave a long tail. Do not close up the hole so you will be able to attach the eyes..

- Wings (make 2)
  - ○ Use MC and loosely ch 6.
  - ○ Rnd 1: Starting in the second ch from hook, work in the back ridge of the loops, sc 2, hdc 2, dc 5 in the back ridge loop of the next chain. Rotate your ch so the front loops are facing up. Starting in the next ch and working in front loops of ch, hdc 2, sc 2 (13 sts).
  - ○ Rnd 2: Sl st 2, sc 9, sl st 2. Fasten off in the first st of rnd 1 and weave in the end.

- Feet (make 2)
  - ○ Use CC1, loosely ch 7.
  - ○ Starting in the second ch from your hook, work in back ridge loops. Sl st 3 * ch 4, starting in the second ch from the hook and working in back ridge loops. Sl st 3.
  - ○ Repeat from the * one more time and continue to work in the back ridge loops of the original ch 7, sl st 3.
  - ○ Fasten off and leave a long tail.

- Comb
  - ○ Using CC2, loosely ch 4.
  - ○ Begin in the second ch from the hook and work in the back ridge loops, sl st 1, ch 3, sl st in base of ch 3, sl st 1, ch 4, sl st in base of ch 4, sl st 1, ch 3, sl st in base of ch 3.

- Fasten and leave a long tail.
- Waddle
  - Using CC2, loosely ch 4 and sl st in the fourth ch from your hook.
  - Fasten off. Leave a long tail.
- Tail Feathers
  - Using MC, make a 7 st adjustable ring.
  - *Sl st 1, ch 5 to 8 sts, sl st in base of ch.
  - Repeat from * six more times to create seven feathers of varying lengths.
  - Fasten and leave a long tail.
- Assembly
  - Attach the plastic eyes between rounds 13 and 14 of the body and place them with 3 or 4 sts between the eyes.
  - Close the hole found at the top of the head. If you have chosen to go with black felt, you can either sew or glue these on. Using a scrap of black, you can sew 2 whort sts above each eye for some eyebrows.
  - Using CC1, make six or seven satin stitches. (Start by drawing the yarn through the surface of your work to make a beak on your chicken.) Place these horizontally between the eyes, then sew the waddle under the bottom of the beak you just made.
  - Sew the comb to the top of the head and over the hole you recently closed.
  - Pinch the bottom half of the back of the body with your fingers. Almost like giving your little

chicken a wedgie. Secure this with three or four running stitches to make a tail shape. Sew the tail feathers to the middle of the tail shaping.

- ○ With the right side of the wings facing out, sew the round ends of the wings to the shoulder area.
- ○ Sew the feet to the bottom of the body.

Rooster

Key:

- Ch: Chain stitch
- Sl st: Slip stitch
- Sc: Single crochet
- Hdc: half double crochet

What You Will Need:

- Yarn: All yarns will be DK weight.
    - d. MC approximately 20 yds in brown
    - e. A approximately 10 yds in white
    - f. B approximately 5 yds in yellow
    - g. C approximately 5 yds in red
    - h. D approximately 5 yds in blue or green
- Hook: E hook
- 6 mm black plastic eyes with safety backings
- Tapestry needle
- Stuffing
- Stitch markers (optional)

Size:

- Approximately 3 inches tall and 2 inches long

Instructions:

- Body
  - Using MC, make an 8 st adjustable ring (see chapter 5).
  - Rnd 1: Sc 2 in each st around (16 sts).
  - Rnd 2: *Sc 3, sc 2 in next st. Repeat from the * three more times (20 sts).
  - Rnd 3: *Sc 1, sc 2 in next st. Repeat from the * nine more times (30 sts).
  - Rnds 4 - 8: Sc 30.
  - Rnd 9: * Sc 1, sc 2 tog. Repeat from the * nine more times (20 sts).
  - Rnd 10: Sc 20. Change to color A
  - Rnd 11: * Sc 3, sc 2 tog. Repeat from * three more times (16 sts).
  - Rnds 12 - 16: Sc 16
  - Stuff body,
  - Rnd 17: Sc 2 tog eight times (8 sts).
  - Fasten. Leave a long tail. You can close up the hole unless you still need to attach the plastic eyes.
- Eyespots (make 2)
  - Using C, make an 8 st adjustable ring.
  - Sl st in the first st of adjustable ring and gently pull partially closed. (Do not close the hole at the center of this adjustable ring completely.) Cut yarn, leaving a long tail.
- Wings (make 2)
  - Using MC, loosely ch 6.

- Rnd 1: Begin in the second ch from the hook and work in the back ridge of loops, sc 2, hdc 2, dc 5 in the back ridge loop of next ch. rotate ch so front loops are facing up. Start in next ch and work in front loops of ch, hdc 2, sc 2 (13 sts)
- Rnd 2: Sl st 2, sc 9, sl st 2 (13 sts).
- Fasten off in the first st of rnd 1 and weave in the end.
- Feet (make 2)
  - Use B and loosely ch 7.
  - Starting in the second ch from your hook, work in the back ridge loops. Sl st 3, *ch 4, starting in the second ch from your hook work in the back ridge loops. Sl st 3. Repeat from * one more time.
  - Continue working in the back ridge loops of the original ch 7, sl st 3.
  - Fasten leaving a long tail.
- Comb
  - Using C, loosely ch 5.
  - Starting in the second ch from your hook and working in the back ridge loops, sl st 1, ch 3, sl st in base of ch 3, *sl st 1, ch 4, al st in base of ch 4. Repeat from * 1 more time, sl st 1, ch 3 sl st in base of the ch 3.
  - Fasten, leaving a long tail.
- Double Waddle
  - Use C and loosely ch 4.
  - Sl st in fourth ch from your hook, ch 4, sl st in fourth ch from hook.

- ○ Fasten and leave a long tail.
- Small Tail Feathers
  - ○ Using D, make a 7 st adjustable ring. *Sl st 1, ch 8 to 10 sts, sl st in base st of ch.
  - ○ Repeat from the * six additional times to create seven feathers of varying lengths.
  - ○ Fasten and leave a long tail.
- Long Tail Feathers
  - ○ Using D, make a 7 stitch adjustable ring.
  - ○ *Sl st 1, ch 12 to 15 sts, sl st in base st of ch.
  - ○ Repeat from * six more times to create seven feathers of varying lengths.
  - ○ Fasten and leave a long tail.
- Assembly
  - ○ Slip an eyespot over the post of a plastic eye and then tighten the eyespot ring. (You will perform this twice.) Install the plastic eyes between rnds 14 and 15 with 3 or 4 sts between the eyes. Use the leftover yarn tails to sew the edges of the eyespots in place.
  - ○ Close the hole found at the top of the head. Using B, make 6 or 7 satin sts between the eyespots for the beak.
  - ○ Sew the waddle under the bottom of the beak.
  - ○ Sew the comb to the top of the head and over the hole you recently closed.
  - ○ Just as you did with the hen, pinch the bottom half of the back of the body with your fingers and secure shaping with three or four running stitches to form a tail shape.

- Stack the long tail feathers on top of the short tail feathers; sew both sets of them to the middle of your tail shaping area.
- With the right side facing out, sew the round end of the wings to the shoulders.
- Sew on the feet to the bottom of the body.

Chick

Key:

- Ch: Chain stitch
- Sl st: Slip stitch
- Sc: Single crochet
- Hdc: half double crochet
- Bl: back loop

What You Will Need:

- Yarn: All yarns will be DK weight.
  - i. MC approximately 15 yds in yellow
  - j. CC approximately 2 yds in dark yellow or orange
- Hook: E hook
- 4 mm black plastic eyes with safety backings
- Tapestry needle
- Stuffing
- Stitch markers (optional)

Size:

- Approximately 1 ½ inches tall and 1 ¼ inches long

Instructions:

- Body
  - Using MC, make a 6 st adjustable ring.
  - Rnd 1: Sc 3, sc 2 in next st, sc 3 in next st, sc 2 in next st (10 stitches).
  - Rnd 2: Sc 3, sc 2 in each of the next 7 sts (17 sts).
  - Rnd 3: In bl, sc 17.
  - Rnds 4-5: Sc 17
  - Rnd 6: Sc 2 tog, *sc 1, sc 2 tog. Repeat from the * four more times (11 sts).
  - Rnd 7: Sc 1, *sc 3, sc 2 tog. Repeat from the * one more time (9 sts).
  - Rnds 8-10: Sc 9
  - Stuff the body. Fasten, leaving a long tail. Do not close up the hole until you have attached the plastic eyes.
- Wings (make 2)
  - Using the MC, make an 8 st adjustable ring. DO NOT join the last st to the first st. Fasten, leave a long tail.
- Assembly
  - Install the plastic eyes between rnds 8 and 9 and main one or two stitches between the eyes. Close the hole found at the top of the head.
  - Use CC to make four or five satin stitches between the eyes to represent the beak.
  - Sew wings to the side of the body.
  - Use the fringe technique (chapter 8) and the MC. Cut four pieces measuring 3 inches long. Attach one piece to the top of the head and the

remaining three pieces in a tight grouping to the lower back of the body to represent the tail.

- ○ Use your tapestry needle to separate the yarn strands and scissors to trim and shape the fuzz.

Miscellaneous

Crochet Coffee Cozy Sleeve

We all enjoy those double mocha lattes, don't we? This quick project will allow you to make a cute little seater for your hot coffees. Have fun. This will be the envy of all your coffee drinking fans.

Key:

- Ch: Chain stitch
- Sl st: Slip stitch
- SC: Single crochet
- Hdc: Half double crochet

What You Will Need:

- Yarn: Chunky, try Bernat Softee Chunky yarn. Pick your favorite color!
- Hook: 9mm N hook
- Time: 10-15 minutes

Instructions:

1. Row 1: Ch 20, sl st to join into ring
2. Rows 2-5: Ch 1, then hdc around (20 stitches) sl st to join
3. Row 6: Sc around. Weave in any ends.

Crochet Heart

You can always hand these out for Valentine's Day or include one in your kid's lunch to show your love and support. Sew one in behind a button! These are versatile because you can use any weight yarn and just match the hook. For example, are you using bulky yarn? Use an M hook. Want a tiny heart? Use sock yarn and a D hook. Worsted weight hearts can be crocheted with an I hook.

Key:

- Ch: Chain stitch
- Sl st: Slip stitch
- Sc: Single crochet
- Hdc: Half double crochet
- Dc: Double crochet

What You Will Need:

- Yarn: Worsted weight, 4 yards. Can be white, pink, or red.
- Hook: 5.5 mm I hook
- Tapestry needle

Instructions:

1. Begin with your slip knot, then ch 4. Join with a sl st. Turn your work so the slip knot is at the back of your work.
2. Row 1. ch 1 then sc into the center of the ring 10 times. Join with sl st. (You should have 11 stitches around your circle.

3. Row 2. Skip the turning chain and make your first dc into the first sc from row 1.
4. Dc then ch 1 a total of two times.
5. Hdc then ch 1 two times.
6. Dc, ch 1
7. Hdc, then ch 1, two times
8. Dc, ch 1, two times
9. Sl st the last two stitches

You should have a total of 19 stitches around the circle, which should look more like a heart.

1. Row 3: Ch 1 for turning chain. Sc 8 times, working your sc into the stitches instead of the gaps from the chain stitches in the previous row. Sc 2 into the chain before the dc stitch once. Sc crochet nine times. Sl st into the last stitch.
2. Cut your yarn leaving about 6 inches. Secure the last stitch, and don't forget to weave in your ends using your tapestry needle toward the indent. This will help with the heart shape.

Crochet Star

Experiment with adding these to your projects. You can also experiment with different yarns and make little delicate versions for baby projects.

Key:

- Ch: Chain stitch
- Sl st: Slip stitch
- Htr: Half treble
- Tr: treble

What You Will Need:

- Yarn: Choose depending upon project
- Hook: Compatible hook for your yarn choice
- Tapestry needle

Instructions:

1. Ch 3, htr 10 in third ch from your hook. Join with a sl st to your first htr. (You should have a total of 10 stitches.
2. Ch 1, *(dc 1, htr 1, tr 1) in the first stitch, ch 2, (tr 1, htr 1, dc 1) in the next st. Repeat from * around and join with a sl st to your first dc.
3. Block to keep your points sharp!

Chapter 8: Helpful Information

There is always some helpful information that you need to refer to quickly. I have tried to gather some of the most pertinent for you.

Hook Chart

Metric is the most accurate measurement when you are picking out your hooks.

Metric	US Number	US Letter	UK Old
2.00 mm	0	-	14
2.25 mm	1	B	13
2.50 mm	1 ½	-	12
2.75 mm	2	C	12
3.00 mm	3	-	11
3.25 mm	3	D	10
3.50 mm	4	E	9
3.75 mm	5	F	9
4.00 mm	6	G	8
4.50 mm	7	-	7
5.00 mm	8	H	6
5.50 mm	9	I	5
6.00 mm	10	J	4

6.50 mm	10 1/2	K	3
7.00 mm	-	-	2
7,50 mm	-	-	1
8.00 mm	11	L	0
9.00 mm	23	N	00
10.00 mm	25	P	000
15 mm	19	-	-

The Gauge

When you get into garments, your gauge will play an important role in dictating how well a garment will fit. You should be making a gauge swatch before you make anything.

'Gauge' actually refers to the number of stitches and rows found within a given width and length of a crochet fabric. Each crochet pattern will include a recommended gauge for the yarn selected to make your item. It is very important that you match this gauge exactly so your work comes out the correct size.

- Choosing the correct gauge. The measurements are usually defined as x amount of stitches and x amount of rows per 4 inches of measurement. Other information may include a measurement that is taken across one or more pattern repeats. Ensuring that your work displays the suggested gauge will help your piece be neither heavy nor too stiff, nor too floppy with loose stitching. Your yarns may also quote a recommended gauge. If you are planning to use a different yarn than indicated by your pattern it would be an excellent idea to work up a sample gauge.

- Determining gauge. Your choice of yarn will affect the size and brand of the crochet hook you use as well as the stitch pattern and the gauge of an individual crocheter. No two people will crochet in the exact same gauge even if you hand them the exact same hook and yarn. The way you hold the yarn, the way it travels through your fingers, and how you hold your hook will all affect the outcome of how your stitches produce a gauge. Crochet fabric will have less give than a piece of similar construction that is knitted. You will find that items like purses, socks, mittens, or hats will often work to a tighter gauge than items like scarves, shawls, garments, or afghans.

- Making and measuring your gauge swatch. Read your pattern instructions because they will always give you a recommended gauge. You will want to work your gauge in the exact yarn that you will use for your project. The size of this should be generous and roughly sized at about 6-8 inches wide. You should choose an appropriate number of foundation chain stitches to support your stitch pattern. You will work in the required pattern stitch until the piece measures approximately 6-8 inches long. Your next step will be to fasten off the yarn and block the swatch using a method suited to your yarn's composition. Allow your blocked piece to dry.

  a. Lay your swatch right side up on a flat surface and use a ruler to measure 4 inches horizontally across a row of stitches. By using two pins, mark this measurement by inserting two pins exactly 4 inches apart. Note the number of stitches between the pins.

b. Turning your work 90°, use your ruler as in the previous step and measure across 4 inches. Make a note of the number of rows found between the pins.

c. When you are working a specified stitch pattern, the gauge information may be shown as a multiple of the pattern rather than a number of stitches and rows. In this instance, you will count repeats of your pattern in between the pins instead of the number of stitches and rows.

d. There is a tool that will gauge your stitch rather than a ruler that has a small cutout window in the lower left-hand corner. The window in this tool, however, only measures 2 inches instead of 4.

- Adjusting gauge. Should you find that you have more stitches than a given gauge, your gauge is running too tight, try making a new swatch with a hook that is the next size larger. Obviously, if you have fewer stitches than a suggested gauge swatch, your stitches are too loose. If so, make a new swatch with a hook one size smaller. Block the new swatch as before and measure the gauge. Repeat this process until your gauge matches what is indicated in the pattern.

- Measuring a block. A block gauge is taken as a finished measurement after your blocked piece has dried. Blocks can be measured in different ways according to the piece's shape.

    e. A square block is measured across the center.

    f. A hexagonal block is measured from side to side or point to point. It will depend upon your pattern's instructions.

    g. A round block should be measured across the diameter.

h. A triangle block should be measured across the base (the widest part).

i. An octagonal block should be measured from side to side or along one edge. The measurement you take will depend upon your instructions in the pattern.

How to Block

What you will need to block your swatch:

- A water source. This can be a sink, bucket, spray bottle, or steam*.

- Rust-proof pins. T Pins are great to use because they offer stability to your piece.

- Blocking board. These are not mandatory, but I feel they are indispensable because of the grid lines provided that help you keep your lines straight, and in the long run, a huge time saver! You can always use your ironing board or a towel covering things like pillows, couch cushions, your mattress; however, please keep in mind that some yarns may bleed

- *I love the steamers, and a hand-held device will probably run you about $35.

If time is important, steaming is by far the quickest method. Should your pattern be more of a lacy stitch, soaking it will provide you with the best accuracy. If you want to use a technique somewhere in the middle, then spray blocking might be the right way for you.

Wet Block

1. Measure your swatch size pre-blocking.
2. Submerge your swatch in a cool water bath until completely wet. Gently squeeze out any excess water. One great method to remove water is to roll your piece in a clean towel and squeeze. Never twist or wring your hand-stitched fabrics.
3. Pin the fabric to a blocking board. Use blocking wires or as many pins as you find necessary to keep your edges straight, avoiding any waves in your edges.
4. Allow to dry completely while pinned. If you remove before the fabric is completely dry, your measurements will be inaccurate. Remove your pins and allow your swatch to relax. The longer you can let it sit, the better. Several hours is sufficient.

5. Give your piece a gentle shake without pulling it. Measuring your piece after it relaxes is the final message or your gauge.

Steam Block

1. Measure your pre-blocked swatch.
2. Pin the swatch to a blocking board. Use blocking wires or pins to keep your edges straight and to avoid any wrinkles or waves in the edges.
3. Pass your steamer or iron (steam setting only) over the fabric, but take care to not touch the hot surface to your swatch. Make sure that the yarn is fully penetrated.
4. Allow to dry completely while pinned. If you remove before the fabric is completely dry, your measurements will be inaccurate. Remove your pins and allow your swatch to relax. The longer you can let it sit before attempting to assemble them, the better. Several hours is sufficient.
5. Give your piece a gentle shake without pulling it. Measuring your piece after it relaxes is the final message or your gauge.

Assembling and Finishing

It's important to finish off your yarn ends neatly and attach seams so that your piece lies neat and professional-looking. With your yarn ends secured, they will not unravel during periods of wear and laundering. Always strive to fasten your ends off as neatly as possible so they do not show through to the front of your work.

Dealing With Yarn Ends

- Finish a yarn end on the top edge by threading the end into a large-eyed needle. Take the yarn through several stitches on the wrong side of the crochet. Work stitch by stitch across the top row of your stitches. Trim any remaining yarn.

- Finish a yarn end on the lower edge by drawing your needle through the backs of several stitches on the wrong side. Trim any remaining yarn.

- Darning into the side edges of single crochet work. You can finish a yarn end by darning it into a side edge of a single crochet. Take the yarn through several rows on the wrong side of your crochet work. Trim any remaining yarn.

- Darning into the side edges of a double crochet. You can finish a yarn end by darning it through two or three end stitches on the backside of your crochet work. Work your ends in stitch by stitch and over the two or three stitches into each row end. Trim any remaining yarn.

- Finishing yarn ends on a stripe pattern. There may come a time when you need to darn yarn ends for more than one color. You will need to take care and pay a little more attention to avoid any colors showing through another. Only thread your needle with one color and darn it into the wrong side of the same color. Repeat with any other color.

- Finishing multiple ends. When working with several strands of yarn, you can use any method, but always treat each yarn end separately. By doing this, you will only do one strand at a time. Trim any ends.

- Finishing the ends when you worked with slippery yarns will benefit you more if you make a series of several back stitches on the wrong side. This acts as an anchor for your end. Trim any ends.
- Finishing the ends of ribbon yarn works best if you pin the yarn end down the edge of the crochet. Use a matching sewing thread to stitch the ribbon in. secure in place. Trim.

Tassels

Making a throw pillow or a great hat, and it's missing a little something? A tassel might just be what you need, and they are a great way to use up any extra yarn you have leftover.

1. First, cut two 12 in lengths of yarn and set them aside.
2. Wind your yarn around a solid object, for example, a sturdy book that represents twice the desired length of the finished tassel. The more wraps you make around your object, the chunkier your tassel will appear.
3. Next, remove the wraps from the object and using one end, tie the wraps together securely around the middle.
4. Fold the wraps in half and wind the end of yarn around the top to create the head of the tassel. Tie the ends off to secure.
5. Cut the loops of yarn and trim to desired length and to create a neat finish.

Fringe

What a great way to make a fun finish to your projects! Fringe can be used on afghans, pillows, scarves, and any number of fun things.

1. Just like when making a tassel, you are going to want to wind lengths of yarn around a book or some other

study object, but it should be the desired length of your fringe.

2. Wrap as many lengths as you need and cut at one end only. Remove the book or object, but keep the fold in the middle of the strands.

3. You can attach these to your project by using a hook to draw the folded middle of a strand through a stitch located at the edge of your project. Make a short loop, then remove your hook and use it to pull the ends through the loop. Tighten, secure and repeat across the desired edge.

Stitching Seams

- Back stitch seam
    1. Place the pieces to be joined together with the right sides facing each other. Pin them together by inserting the pins at right angles to the edge of the work. Thread a tapestry needle with a matching yarn, then secure the yarn end making two or three stitches at the beginning of the seam. Take the yarn through both layers of crochet and over the edge.
    2. Working one or two stitches away from the edge, make a row of back stitches working from right to left. With each stitch, bring the needle through only a short distance in front of the previous stitch. Take it back through from where the previous stitch emerged. Finish off your thread end and secure it.

- Chain stitch seam
    1. This is a stitched version of your slip stitch seam. Begin by placing the pieces that need to be joined together with the right sides facing.

Pin them together and insert the pins at right angles to the edge. Thread a tapestry needle with matching yarn and work a row of chain stitches. Remember to position the stitches close to the edge.

- Woven seam
    2. Place the pieces you have to be joined side by side on a flat surface. The right edges should be facing upward, and the row ends should touch. Thread your tapestry needle with matching yarn and work a vertical row of evenly spaced stitches in a loose zigzag pattern from edge to edge. Work a stitch through the right-hand block and pull the yarn through.
    3. Work the next stitch through the piece on the left and pull your yarn through. Take care to carefully adjust the tension of your yarn every two or three stitches as you go along.
- Woven seam across upper edges.
    4. Place two pieces to be attached side by side on a flat surface with the wrong sides facing upward and the top edges touching.
    5. Thread a yarn needle with matching colored yarn and work a horizontal row of evenly spaced stitches through your chains. Work steadily from edge to edge in the same way you would do in the chain stitch seams found above. Carefully adjust the tension of the stitches so you have no puckers or waves as you work on pulling the edges together.
- Whip-stitched seam
    6. Begin by placing the pieces to be joined with the right sides facing, but do not pin them. Hold the

pieces together and place your left index finger between layers. Work, making a series of small stitches over the edges and picking up one stitch at a time.

7. Always match the corner stitches at the beginning and end of each seam when whip-stitching your pieces together. Work consistently by going through the outer loops only or through both loops together only.Crocheted Seams

- Slip stitch seam

8. Place the pieces that you want to join together with the right sides facing and pin them together. Insert the pins at right angles to the edge. Then while holding the yarn behind the pieces, insert the hook through both layers of fabric and draw a loop of yarn through both layers, and a loop of yarn through both pieces, and the loop on the hook.

9. Repeat this working from right to left all the way across until you have reached the end. Secure the yarn ends because slip stitch seams tend to unravel easily.

Single Crochet Seam Across Upper Edges

1. Place the pieces you want to join together with the right sides facing to create a concealed seam. If you want a decorative seam, you can put the wrong sides together. Pin the layers together so that the top edges align. Insert the pins at right angles to the edge.

2. Holding the yarn behind the work, insert your hook through a pair of corresponding chains from each piece. Work a row of single crochet

(one single crochet into each pair of aligned chains.

Single Crochet Seam Across Row Ends

1. As before, place your pieces' right sides together and pin. Hold your yarn behind your work and insert the hook through both layers of fabric, working a single crochet stitch. Continue working in single crochet stitches all the way across and keeping those stitches close to the edge.

2. When working on single crochet fabric, work one stitch into every row end. If double crochet fabric, work two or three stitches per row depending on the yarn weight. If working with other stitch patterns, make sure to space the seam stitches evenly, making sure that your work remains flat without any waves or puckering.

- Single crochet and chain seam
    1. Place pieces you want to join the right sides together and pin together with the pins at right angles to your edge. Hold the yarn behind the work to be joined, insert the hook through both layers and work a single crochet stitch at the beginning of the seam. Work a chain followed by another single crochet stitch placed just a short distance from the first.
    2. Repeat this pattern along the entire edge and continue to alternate between a single crochet and a chain stitch. Finish your row with a single crochet stitch. Space your stitches out as evenly as possible and as with all the other seams, make sure it remains flat with no puckers.

When Working With Slippery Yarn Tip

1. If you find yourself working with a slippery yarn, when you finish your final row, try working one chain stitch at the end to help lock the yarn in place. You can then cut your yarn and pull on the final loop to tighten your final row. Pull gently to tighten your final chain before you tie off and weave in the end.

Laundering Crochet Tips

1. You are given washing and pressing instructions on the yarn band. That will tell you whether your yarn is machine washable or not.
2. Always put your piece in a zippered mesh laundry bag to prevent it from getting stretched out or snagged on something during your wash cycle.
3. For those pieces that are not machine washable, you can still hand wash them in a mild detergent-free cleaning agent. You will find that most purpose-made wool or fabric shampoos will work ideally, but you should always check to make sure that they do not incorporate any optical brighteners, which would cause your yarn colors to fade. These pieces will need to be rinsed through several changes of water at the same temperature. Never wring out your pieces, instead opting to squeeze out as much surplus water as possible. You can roll the damp item in a towel, and lay it out flat avoiding any direct sunlight.
4. Lacy items will need to be blocked every time they are washed.

Storing Your Crochet

Dust and dirt can really wreak havoc on your crocheted fabrics, but another enemy of your handiwork is direct sunlight which can cause your beautiful creations to fade. Your yarns can become dry and brittle due to excessive heat, dampness will rot out fibers, and moths can chew on your woolen garments. So how you choose to store your crocheted goods is very important.

Storing yarns or finished goods in bags made of polyethylene will attract dust and dirt particles. Bags made from polyethylene will prevent yarns composed of natural fibers like cotton and linen from breathing. This inability can cause mildew and will weaken or rot your fibers.

Small items can be wrapped in white, acid-free tissue paper or an old white cotton pillowcase. Larger, heavier items can be more of a challenge. But they need to be folded loosely with layers of white acid-free tissue paper in between the folds (you need to make certain that each fold is padded).

All of your items should then be stored in a drawer, closet, or other dark, dry, and moth-free place. It is a good idea to check your items regularly and refold the larger items. Small sachet bags of lavender flowers can help deter moths.

Notebook

When you are beginning, it can be very beneficial to make swatches of your basic stitches so you can refer to them, but another handy idea is to make project notes regarding all your projects. With it, you can store a small amount of yarn swatches in case you need to make a repair.

You can attach your yarn label and make any kind of notation regarding washing instructions. Your sample book should be kept in a box with a lid and stored in a cool, dry place.

Conclusion

I know that learning to crochet can seem a bit daunting at first because, with all the abbreviations, special characters, and new equipment, it can seem like you are learning a new language. In fact, you are. However, it is significantly easier than trying to learn Spanish or Klingon. There are also many interesting facts about crochet and its role in history. Remember the potato famine reference?

This is not just a keep busy hobby for retirees; there are plenty of young people that have learned the many benefits that crochet has to offer and, you can make some lovely stuff!

I am willing to bet that you never knew all the health benefits that one can receive from enjoying crochet, and it not only benefits you but can enhance your bond with your child while you pass along the tradition.

In chapter 3, I described many of the skills you will need to get your new hobby kickstarted, and you now know not only how to hold a hook and your yarn, but how to work some of those basic stitches that will be your foundation as you excel at your craft. By the end of this chapter, I am positive that you will be anxious to begin your first project.

Since I have armed you with plenty of basic stitch knowledge and provided variations as well, your know-how has increased, and you feel ready to get on with some of the more detailed stitches. If you weren't aware that you could join embroidery along with your new hobby, I have even mentioned which stitches you can successfully use in conjunction with your work.

In addition to all the well-known libraries of stitches, I have included an introduction to one of the newest stitches to come along in some time, the corner-to-corner stitch.

I have successfully given you many little in-depth details in regards to step-by-step instructions on how to perform some little-known techniques like how to make adjustable rings, so you don't have noticeable holes in some of your projects.

I have even added some finishing touch instructions that can add that extra boost to your beginning crochet projects and make you look like you have been practicing crochet forever. Now you can add those neat edgings and cover your own buttons, making everyone wonder how you got so advanced.

Chapter 7 contains many fun projects that I just know you cannot wait to get started on, and even if you don't use them for yourself, they can be donated, given away as gifts, or bring a smile to a child in need. (I am especially fond of the little toy chicken family!)

Besides patterns, I have given you some cute embellishments to add under a button or sew on a project to give it something special.

Last but not least, I have included many little tidbits of information on how to determine a gauge for your project, block your pieces, the different techniques on how to stitch your pieces together, laundering, and storage tips. For fun, I have even thrown in finishing your pieces off with tassels and fringe.

Being a good crocheter is not about being perfect; it's all about being creative and self-expression. The more you learn, the better you will become because it's all about confidence. We were all complete novices once, but we learn and develop a technique that is ours, and many of us even go on to design our own creations.

I know that you have a bright future in the creation of many wonderful things. So grab your crochet hook and your favorite yarn and dive right in!

References

CreatiKnitCreatiKnitFollow. (n.d.). *How to make a slip knot for knitting, or crochet!* Instructables. Retrieved May 13, 2021, from https://www.instructables.com/How-to-make-a-Slip-Knot-for-Knitting-or-Crochet/

Crochet. (2020, May 27). Wikipedia. https://en.wikipedia.org/wiki/Crochet

Crochet cuffed baby booties pattern. (2012, October 1). Repeat Crafter Me. https://www.repeatcrafterme.com/2012/10/crochet-cuffed-baby-booties-pattern.html

Eaton, J. (2004). Crochet basics: *All you need to know to get hooked on crochet.* Barron's Educational Series.

Eaton, J. (2007). *200 crochet tips, techniques & trade secrets: An Indispensable Resource for technical know-how and trouble-shooting Tips.* St. Martin's Press.

Hiatt, M. (n.d.). *Crocheting can improve your memory, concentrations, and sense of calm.* Better Homes & Gardens. Retrieved May 12, 2021, from https://www.bhg.com/syndication/crocheting-improve-memory-concentration-and-calm/?fbclid=IwAR32R0I-FAcFzJsVdYuC6VpwQBb7dURiFqobg7C_63-67I8elVx1eKuJ8Xg&utm_campaign=bhg_mybhg&utm_content=link_topcontent&utm_medium=social&utm_source=facebook.com&utm_term=2BEBB234-1E67-11E9-BF81-0AFC4F017A06

Jessica. (2018, September 25). *10-minute beginner crochet coffee cozy sleeve (a free pattern)*. Db2. https://www.domesticbliss2.com/2018/09/beginner-crochet-coffee-cozy.html/

Kreiner, M. (2015). *Crochet a farm: 19 cute-as-can-be barnyard creations*. Martingale, Create With Confidence.

Leinhauser, J. (n.d.). *How to read a crochet pattern | welcome to the craft yarn council.* Www.craftyarncouncil.com. Retrieved May 14, 2021, from https://www.craftyarncouncil.com/standards/how-to-read-crochet-pattern

Marks, R. (2019). *Crochet guild of america*. Crochet.org. https://www.crochet.org/page/CrochetHistory

Morgan, J. (2020, May 3). *Crochet facts - 30 - Amazing things - I bet you never knew!* Https://Crochetpenguin.com/. https://crochetpenguin.com/crochet-facts/

Morgan, L. (n.d.). *Crochet hook conversion chart*. Leonie Morgan. Retrieved May 17, 2021, from https://www.leoniemorgan.com/wp-content/uploads/2017/02/Crochet-Hook-Conversion-Chart.pdf

Pionk, J. (2017, January 30). *How to crochet - Front post treble crochet* (fptr) (photo & video tutorial). A Crocheted Simplicity. https://www.acrochetedsimplicity.com/how-to-crochet-front-post-treble-crochet-fptr-photo-video-tutorial/

Red Heart Design Team. (n.d.). *How to teach children to crochet | yarnspirations.* Www.yarnspirations.com. Retrieved May 12, 2021, from https://www.yarnspirations.com/rh-20180724-how-to-teach-children-to-crochet.html

Sea breeze tank top - Free crochet pattern + video tutorial. (2019, May 10). For the Frills. https://forthefrills.com/sea-breeze-tank-top-free-crochet-pattern/

Shrimpton, S. (2020). *Modern crochet bible: Over 100 techniques for contemporary crochet.* David & Charles Publishers.

Smith, E. (1897). *Memoirs of a highland lady, etc.* Edinburgh: Privately Printed By R. & R. Clark. (Original work published 1797)

Solovay, A. (2019a, April 27). *Add a simple edging to your crochet with the shell stitch.* The Spruce Crafts. https://www.thesprucecrafts.com/simple-shell-stitch-crochet-edging-pattern-978649

Solovay, A. (2019b, May 29). *Learn if crocheting is the right craft hobby for your personality.* The Spruce Crafts. https://www.thesprucecrafts.com/is-crochet-right-for-you-979066

Sterling Publishing Company. (2004). *Crocheting school: A complete course.* Sterling Pub. Co.

Swatman, R. (2016, February 2). *Indian women make the largest crochet blanket ever then donate it to charity.* Guinness World Records. https://www.guinnessworldrecords.com/news/2016/

2/indian-women-make-largest-crochet-blanket-ever-then-donate-it-to-charity-415230

Velasquez, R. (2020, July 10). *Blocking a gauge swatch: A guide on how and why • RV designs*. RV Designs. https://www.rebeccavelasquez.com/swatch-blocking/

White, S. (2020, March 27). *A simple guide to understanding yarn weights*. The Spruce Crafts. https://www.thesprucecrafts.com/understanding-yarn-weights-2117311

Wiatr, J. (2017, January 20). *7 (surprising) health benefits of crocheting*. AllFreeCrochet.com. https://www.allfreecrochet.com/Tips-for-Crochet/Crochet-Health-Benefits

Photography Resources

Cotta, M. (2021a). https://www.pexels.com/photo/white-brown-and-black-striped-textile-6462892/

Cotta, M. (2021b). https://www.pexels.com/photo/art-pattern-texture-design-6463348/

Cottonbro. (2020). https://www.pexels.com/photo/person-holding-blue-yarn-roll-3942933/

Lusina, A. (2020a, June 29). Https://Www.pexels.com/Photo/Yarn-Ball-And-Needle-Placed-On-Bed-Near-Opened-Magazine-4792090/.

Lusina, A. (2020b). https://www.pexels.com/photo/pink-yarn-on-gray-cozy-sofa-4792062/

Michaelyne, M. (2021a).
https://www.pexels.com/photo/fashion-pattern-texture-knitwear-7156841/

Michaelyne, M. (2021b).
https://www.pexels.com/photo/white-brown-and-black-striped-textile-6462892/

Overbye, N. (2021).
https://www.pexels.com/photo/fashion-rope-craft-homemade-6542289/

Stock, C. (2020a).
https://www.pexels.com/photo/person-holding-purple-crochet-hook-and-white-yarn-3945638/

Stock, C. (2020b).
https://www.pexels.com/photo/person-holding-a-crochet-hook-3945636/